DOUBLE MEASURES

DOUBLE
MEASURES

THE GUARDIAN
BOOK OF DRINKING

EDITED BY
RICHARD NELSSON

guardianbooks

Published by Guardian Books 2008

2 4 6 8 10 9 7 5 3 1

Copyright © Guardian News and Media Ltd 2008

Richard Nelsson has asserted his right under the Copyright, Designs
and Patents Act 1988 to be identified as the editor of this work

First published in Great Britain in 2008 by
Guardian Books
119 Farringdon Road
London EC1R 3ER
www.guardianbooks.co.uk

A CIP catalogue record for this book is available from the British Library

ISBN: 978-0-85265-105-6

Designed by Two Associates
Typeset by seagulls.net

Printed in Great Britain by TJ International, Padstow, Cornwall

CONTENTS

Introduction
6

1 Sense and insensibility
10

2 Brewers under siege
34

3 Licence to kill
60

4 Behind closed doors
86

5 Community spirit
114

6 From grain to grape
132

7 The light stuff
156

8 The more, the merrier
178

9 Drowning discontent
208

10 This plastered isle
232

References
268

Index
269

INTRODUCTION

EVER since humans settled down to live into organised societies, alcoholic drink has played a major role in the rituals of everyday life. It is used to celebrate births and to commiserate at wakes, as a source of nutrition, a religious symbol and, most commonly, the lubricant that eases social occasions. It is, of course, also blamed for many of society's problems: newspapers have been reporting on alcohol-related violence and helping fuel moral panic over binge drinking for more than 200 years.

This collection looks at drink through the eyes of *Guardian* (and formerly *Manchester Guardian*) writers and includes everything from the politics of drink, and what and where people imbibe, to how to cope with the effects of the over-indulgent moment.

The first article in *Double Measures* dates from 1821, the year the *Manchester Guardian* was founded by John Edward Taylor, a young cotton trader and part-time journalist. The origins of the paper though can be traced back to March 30 1819 when, after he had won a libel case brought against him by a leading Tory, a friend told him, "It is now plain you have the elements of public work in you. Why don't you start a newspaper?" Five months later, Taylor witnessed the notorious Peterloo Massacre, when a cavalry charge on a demonstration demanding MPs for Manchester left 11 people dead. The young reporter's cool, analytical accounts for the London papers helped to make Peterloo a national scandal.

In the wake of this Taylor, whose political views were those of a reformer, persuaded 11 friends to lend him the money needed set up a newspaper. The first edition, published as a weekly on a Saturday, appeared on May 5

1821 and after going twice weekly in the 1830s, the *Manchester Guardian* became a daily paper in 1855. Charles Prestwich Scott (always known as CP Scott) became editor in 1872 and under his direction the provincial paper achieved national and international recognition. "Manchester" was not, however, dropped from the masthead until 1959 and, a few years later, most of the editorial departments moved to London.

From the very beginning the paper was admired for its honest reporting and, during the 19th century, it developed a reputation for having a liberal, independent, and occasionally eccentric spirit. It was also noted, however, for its sober, nonconformist colour – not, it must be said, an obvious source for drink-friendly articles.

This seemed to be confirmed when I began trawling through the *Guardian*'s digital archive and discovered on the top right-hand corner of the very first front page an advert for a just published book that offered, "A new system of vegetable cookery: with an introduction recommending abstinence from animal food and intoxicating liquors." This was immediately followed by a verse from the Bible warning that it was not good to drink intoxicating wine.

Meanwhile searches for drink-related articles in the earlier years of the paper delivered numerous long reports of temperance meetings, carefully listing who attended and what was said. The *Manchester Guardian* was certainly sympathetic to the temperance movement, which was dedicated to promoting moderation in the use of intoxicating liquor. It saw a reduction in drinking as a means of improving the social conditions of the working classes rather than taking the view that all drink was evil and thereby calling for total abstinence. Delving deeper into the archive, a treasure-trove of stories emerged. There were stories about gin palaces, the effects of indulging in absinthe (the green fairy), or hunting for illegal poteen distilleries. The beginning of the 20th century saw the appearance of the Miscellany column comprising short, often quirky, pieces sometimes involving the revival of memories or curious modern parallels. The column was to appear in various guises until the late 1960s and so provided a valuable source of material.

Apart from leading articles, the paper also offered serious and witty comment on the drink issues of the day while longer, in-depth features on subjects such as the effects of prohibition in the US began to appear. By the 1950s it regularly carried long features and surveys on wine, and by the 1970s it had John Arlott as wine critic and Richard Boston writing probably the first ever dedicated beer column in a national newspaper.

The articles are arranged in chronological order, with major pieces of drink-related legislation forming a basic timeline. Beyond this there was no particular agenda when selecting the material other than to reflect how social and cultural influences have determined changing tastes in alcoholic beverages over the past 180 years or so.

I would like to thank Lisa Darnell, Mike McNay, Polly Pattullo, Tim Radford, Mariam Yamin at the *Guardian* and *Observer*'s Newsroom archive, and everyone in the paper's research and information department. Also, Alan Patrickson, a longstanding drinking companion. Last, but not least, thanks to Fiona, Hannah and Freya for their support and giving me the space to do this.

CHAPTER ONE
SENSE AND
INSENSIBILITY

THE dawn of the 19th century saw Britain trying to shake off the excesses of the drinking of the previous decades. The consumption of gin, or 'Madam Geneva' as it was also known, had ravaged whole sections of society during the first half of the 1700s, and wine and beer were probably at the strongest that the country has ever known.

After banning the import of French brandy and other foreign spirits in 1690, the government deliberately encouraged the domestic distilling of spirits; duties on gin were cut while those of beer were increased. With gin now cheaper than beer, consumption by the urban, often non-working classes rocketed. So much so that by 1742, a population – barely a tenth the size of today's – consumed 19 million gallons of gin, 10 times as much, and indeed stronger, than is drunk today.

The signs outside gin shops inviting customers to be 'Drunk for 1d, dead drunk for 2d' may have been an urban myth, but in 1751 William Hogarth used it in Gin Lane, where he graphically depicted the spirit's lethal consequences. Various Gin Acts were introduced to try to curb this rampant drinking but it wasn't until the 1851 act, which restricted the sale and increased the price, that the rage for gin began to decline.

Strong drink though was still very much part of everyday society. The upper and middle classes consumed excessive amounts of port: prime minister William Pitt the younger, for example, knocked back up to three bottles a day. The 1700s also saw the rise in popularity of porter, a strong, dark beer with a creamy head, thought to have acquired its name from the porters on the streets of London but which became popular with those who did physical work.

Beer consumption rose and the breweries became very powerful, owning many 'tied' drinking establishments; by the beginning of the 19th century they had a considerable parliamentary lobby with scores of brewer MPs. Meanwhile the 1820s saw gin consumption on the rise again, with illegal distilling and smuggling rife.

It was against this background that the Duke of Wellington's Tory government brought in the Beerhouse Act 1830, a piece of legislation that aimed to reduce the power of the big breweries as well attempting to take the traffic and sale of drinks out of the hands of smugglers. The act allowed any householder and ratepayer, who could afford the two-guinea licence fee, to sell beer, ale or porter on their premises, as well as encouraging them to brew their own. Perhaps not surprisingly consumption rocketed and the clergyman-journalist, Reverend Sydney Smith, commented: 'The new Beer Bill has begun its operations. Everybody is drunk. Those who are not singing are sprawling.' Within the year, 24,000 new beer shops had opened across England and Wales (the act wasn't applied to Scotland).

The act also had the effect of generating competition among licensed publicans leading to a growth in 'gin palaces', gaudily decorated public houses with lots of plate glass and illuminated by the newly invented gas lighting. In *Sketches by Boz*, Charles Dickens contrasted the 'light and brilliancy' of the gin palace with the squalor of the surrounding London streets and said they were extremely popular.

In response to this, a temperance movement began to develop. Originally it was concerned with the excessive consumption of spirits and its corrosive effect on the poor rather than a complete rejection of alcohol. But the failure of the Beer Act led some to embrace total abstinence. In September 1832, seven men in Preston signed the first pledge to be alcohol-free including a certain Richard 'Dicky' Turner, who declared his abstinence would be 'tee-tee-total for ever and ever', thus introducing the word teetotal to the world.

Campaigners started to look to the United States for inspiration where, in 1851, Maine was the first state to get all alcohol prohibited; 12 other states followed. However, the *Guardian* carried a piece ridiculing this Maine Law, reporting that drinking continued to carry on behind closed doors. The paper had initially supported the Beer Act and although it was calling for reform it did not support full prohibition.

After the abolition of excise duty on glass in 1845, glass manufacturing became cheaper, which led to a growth in bottling drink. This helped to guarantee the quality of beer and meant that it be could be transported over longer distances. It also allowed the drink to be packaged more attractively, particularly the new lighter and less alcoholic beers, such as India Pale Ale. Meanwhile in a German town called Pilsen, a new style of golden coloured beer called lager began to appear.

Society was moving away from strong port to lighter wines and this was reflected in the budget of 1860 where William Gladstone, the chancellor of the exchequer, reduced duties on table wines. He also introduced the 'Single Bottle' Act which meant that a shopkeeper could sell just one bottle of wine at a time, to a customer, whereas previously it had to be bought wholesale or from a pub. This led to an expansion of claret drinking among the growing middle classes.

* * *

The King's glass

The turn of his Majesty's head, the shape of his hat and clothes, have become quite the fashion in Ireland since the King's visit; every act of the royal personage has found a crowd of admirers; even the manner in which his Majesty drank his wine is imitated in every company by those who wish to have a character as judges of the flavour of Rhenish. The King on public occasions always drank bumpers,* but he kept his glass four times longer to his lips than is ordinarily allowed for swallowing a cheerful glass, and seemed to sip the wine drop by drop, so that the palate had the fullest opportunity of imbibing the flavour of, no doubt, a rare and rich vintage. The King threw his head greatly back as he sipped his glass, but never took the wine from his lips, until he cleared the bumper.

September 22 1821

*BUMPER – *a formal toast drunk with the glass filled to the brim*

* * *

Rum jelly

Among the novelties of the Parisian circles, rum-jelly has become an universal favourite. It is made in the following manner:- To a quart bottle of common white wine take a pound of sugar, which is to be reduced to a syrup, and clarified. Then take an ounce of isinglass,* which put on the fire till it is thoroughly melted, pass it through a cloth, and mix it with the syrup, half warm. When this mixture is nearly cold, pour it into the white wine, and stir it well so as to mix it completely. Then add a spoonful or a spoonful and a half (according to the strength which you desire to give to the jelly) of old Jamaica rum. Stir again this mixture, and pour it into the mould, that it may take the shape in cooling which you design to give it, if intended as a plat for the table, or into glasses, if designed to be handed round at an evening party.

October 6 1821

ISINGLASS – a form of gelatin used to clarify liquor

* * *

THE WINES OF 1825
GERMAN WINES – it is the universal opinion on the Rhine, that the quality of the wine of this year will be very fine, but the quantity will not much exceed an average vintage. The opinion which so commonly prevails in this country, of the necessity of drinking old Rhenish wine, is little known in the country of its production. The wines of 1811 are much esteemed, as well as those of 1822, from the excellence of the vintages; but except these, there is little, commonly no distinction or care, as to the ages of the wines.

It is said by the wine-merchants of Cologne and Coblentz, that the introduction of steamboats on the Upper Rhine (in the establishment of which they have assisted) will materially benefit their trade. The little boatmen who have undertaken hitherto the carriage of the wine to Holland, were never responsible, and seldom trustworthy persons. Besides the slowness of their operations, the wine entrusted to them was often diminished, or deteriorated by a mixture of water; and it has happened that casks for which transmit duty had actually been paid in Holland, have been found full of pure water. The steam-vessels will be enabled to tow down the steamboats laden with wine; and the rapidity of transport, and the absence of risk from dishonesty, must together cause a reduction in price.

FRENCH WINES – Great efforts are said to be made this year to produce a large quantity of sparkling Burgundy, of which a few specimens have already been made, and much esteemed by amateurs. The quality of wine, both in Burgundy and in other parts of France, this year, is said to be good, but the quantity not very great.

The following is an extract of a letter, dated Tours, Oct. 6:- 'This vintage of this year is in high repute, and is considered to be the best which has presented itself for many years past; the consequence is, that the prices are comparatively high. The country is filled with Parisian wine-merchants, who are buying all they can lay their hands on. They are the more induced to do so, because from the excessive heat of the summer the grape has produced a very high-coloured wine, and it will consequently bear a greater mixture. The price of wine, in this country, is four pounds a piece (about 60 gallons) cask included. At Orleans it is only half that price, but there the wine is not so good; further south, the choice wines have risen to an enormous price. I mean the wines of this season. La Fitte has risen to 3,609 francs, to which must be added 800 francs commission for wastage and cellarage, making together 4,400 francs for a tonneau of wine, comprising about four English hogsheads, or, in other words, about £44 sterling the hogshead; so high is the reputation of this year's vintage.'

PORT – By advices from Oporto, dated Sept. 27, we learn that the vintage (for the success of which considerable fears were entertained for some period past, in consequence of the heavy and incessant rains experienced there), will prove a productive one, and it is hoped the quality of the wine will be very superior to what was anticipated. A long letter, giving an account of the general view of the vintage, concludes in the following brief but satisfactory manner:- 'The vintage, after all, will be a famous one; the weather has cleared up just in time for us, and all is going on most prosperously.'

October 22 1825

* * *

Dram drinking

There can, we apprehend, be little doubt that the question of the beer and malt duties will be brought before parliament in the ensuing session; and if so, an interesting discussion will, in all probability, arise, as to the great and alarming increase in dram-drinking.

That the very low price of gin is an evil – that every thing is an evil which increases the temptation to the lower classes of our population to addict themselves to the use of ardent spirits, will not, we think, be denied by any one who has eyes about him in the streets, or who has paid any attention to the evidence which has been taken and published, by successive parliamentary police committees, with respect to the effects of the practice.

We have seen the number of gin-shops in this and the adjoining town, within comparatively a very few years, multiplied at least 50 fold – so fast indeed, that in all probability, unless some alteration take place, there will speedily be hardly a public-house left, which retains its old appearance.

There is no want, therefore, it appears to us, of perfectly valid reasons why dram-drinking should be checked by every measure which it is within the competency of parliament to apply.

There are many persons who do not hesitate to slip cautiously into a spirit-shop and drink a glass of gin (perhaps repeating the practice at different places, very frequently, in the course of a day), who would not allow themselves to be seen sitting in the tap-room of a public-house. This remark is particularly applicable to females, of who, we believe, there is, unfortunately, little doubt the majority of customers of gin-shops consist.

The frightful consequences with which the vice of intemperance is inevitably fraught, render it incumbent on the legislature to discourage it; but in many respects, this is obviously a matter of difficulty. It is, indeed, desirable that the poor should have beverages at command, which may not only assist in repairing the strength exhausted by labour, but serve to promote domestic and social relaxation. Whilst, therefore, we would repress as much as possible the temptations to the use of ardent spirits, we would afford every facility and encouragement for the production and sale to the poor of good and wholesome beer, at as low a rate as a necessary attention to the revenue will admit. It is extremely desirable, also, that in any change that may be made, as much inducement as possible should be held out to lead the poor to take their refreshment of liquor, as well as of food, at home; and thus avoid that danger of temptation to excess, which is involved in a frequent resort to public-houses.

Leader, November 14 1829

* * *

New beer bill
The excise duties on beer will cease on the 10th of next month on which day the new beer act will come into operation. The following is an abstract of it:-

From and after the 10th day of October, 1830, it will be lawful for every person who shall obtain a license of the commissioners, collectors, or supervisors of excise (paying for the same sum of £2.2s) to sell beer, ale, or porter, by retail, in any part of England, in any house of premises specified in such licence; but such licence will not authorise or entitle any party to sell wine or spirits. Penalty for so doing £20, without mitigation.

October 10 1830

* * *

New regulations of beer shops
Sir, – I am glad the magistrates have thought proper to oblige the beer houses to keep their doors closed until one o'clock on the Sunday, for I have seen the beneficial effects of it already in my own neighbourhood; and I feel no doubt but many a poor infatuated man will reap advantage from

it; and that the peace and order of the town generally will be promoted by it.

But I am unable to see why the same regulation should not be extended to the public houses, and especially to the gin shops. If a shopkeeper venture to sell a pound of bread, cheese or bacon, on the Sunday, he is liable to be brought before a magistrate, and punished for breaking the Sabbath; but the gin retailer opens wide his doors on that holy day to sell his pestiferous, yes, both soul and body destroying stuff, the immediate effect of which is to promote Sabbath breaking and drunkenness, with all its consequent disorder, crime and misery; and in this he is countenanced and supported by the same powers that would punish (and in my opinion properly) the shopkeeper for selling his wholesome and necessary articles of food on that day.

I hope such glaring inconsistencies at these will not long disgrace our country. It would, in my opinion be an excellent regulation if both the public houses and gin shops were obliged to close on Saturday nights at the same hour (ten) as the beer shops. Many men upon leaving their work at four o'clock accompany their shop-mates to a beer house, in many instances kept by a fellow workman, and there they remain until ten o'clock, at which time they are turned out; considerably excited with the liquor they have already taken, and they will agree to go together to some public house, and at this place they will spend twice or three times the sum they have spent at all the preceding part of the evening; whilst they are sober many of them are not unmindful that they have but little to spare, if their families must be properly attended to; but by the time at which the beer houses close all prudential consideration have gone, and they remain at the public house regardless of everything but present gratification, until at twelve o'clock they are again turned out, and sent home with the remnant of their wages, at an hour at which the shops are closed and the market over; consequently their wives are obliged to go to the butchers on Sunday morning, if they are to have any butcher's meat for dinner, and to some shop, begging that they may be allowed to purchase that which is necessary for the day. If public houses and spirit vaults were obliged to close at ten o'clock as well as beer houses, very many who do not do it now, would then reach their homes in time for their wives to provide for the ensuing week, and very many would return home with money to expend in procuring real comforts and enjoyments for themselves and families which they now spend in begetting, fostering, and confirming habits of drunkenness.

I sincerely wish that the thinking and respectable part of the community would seriously attend to the exceeding prevalence of intemperance amongst us – the causes of it and its effect: the result would be in most cases deep conviction that it is indeed time for extraordinary measures to be resorted to, and though different opinions are and would be formed as to the best means to check the progress of this degrading vice, and consequently various plans pursued to effect the same, there is no doubt but the general result would be great and extensive good, – I am, sir, yours &c., H.W.

November 8 1834

THE GIN DOCTOR

On one occasion, soon after Mr Williams commenced business, he had mixed up in a vat in the cellar, 200 gallons of gin, putting nothing in it that could in any way injure the constitution of his customers. But to his surprise they began to drop off, one by one, and those who did continue to drink it, declared it was much inferior to what was sold in the neighbourhood. This was a puzzle to Mr Williams; he could not conceive how they could find fault with such a beautiful article as that. However, the puzzle was soon solved, as follows:

A gentleman drove up to the door, one day, in an open carriage, and, giving the reins to his servant, stepped into the gin palace, and called for glass of gin. Being served, he tasted it and sat it down; again he tasted it, and asked if it was the *best*; and, being answered in the affirmative, he shook his head, and remarked, 'It won't do.' Mr Williams here commenced a long story in praise of his gin. 'Yes,' says the gentleman, 'it may be all that you can say of it; but still, I affirm that it won't do.' The other as eagerly inquired, 'Pray *why* won't it do?' The gentleman then, in half whisper, inquired if there were any one in the bar parlour; signifying, at the same time, that, if he might be permitted, he would tell he him *why* it would not do. Being closeted, he began to unfold to Mr Williams that he was a *Gin Doctor*, that with his drugs the gin would be a first-rate article, but that if he persisted in selling gin without being drugged he would soon have to shut up his shop. By way of convincing him of the truth of what he said, he desired Mr Williams to bring him two glasses of gin; then taking from his pocket a small phial, he let a few drops of it fall into one glass, and stirring it with his pencil-case desired him to compare the two. The result was truly astonishing. It was not like the same article. He then urged our friend Williams to give an order, but without success, he called again and again; and it was not till Williams plainly saw, as the man had said, that unless he would use drugs he must soon shut up shop. It was soon noised over the neighbourhood that Williams had the best gin, and then commenced a *run* of business. Williams sometimes smiled to himself when he saw the poor creatures drain the last drop from the glass and smack their lips, saying, 'There now, that was a gin,' well knowing that it was not; but consoling himself with the reflection that he could not sell them the genuine article, and that it was absolutely necessary, in order to pay rents, taxes, servants' wages, &c. that he should sell something.

March 10 1847

* * *

Working of the Maine Law

In 1854 this law was passed by the legislature of the state of Maine; and it has since, with various modifications, found its way into the statute books of Minnesota, Michigan, Massachusetts, Ohio and Connecticut. Mr Charles Lindsey, an influential citizen of Toronto, Canadian commissioner at the French exhibition, proceeded to several of the states where the Maine Law was in operation, to collect evidence. The result of his investigation was published in a series of articles in a Toronto paper, and afterwards as a pamphlet, a copy of which is before us; and certainly his evidence is potent to us as to the utter failure of the law. He shows that it has only served to extend secret drinking; that crime generally, and especially the crimes arising from drunkenness have greatly increased since the introduction of the law; and that in short its influence and effects are most baneful and demoralising. Mr Lindsey first visited Vermont, on a cold December day, and he thus describes what he saw and tasted:

It was about dusk as I arrived at a large hotel, where I found about 50 guests. The company was not more miscellaneous than one usually meets on such occasions.

There was a bar; but it contained neither glass cases nor decanters; neither tumblers nor wine glasses. The porter pump was not there. In short, except a waiter and a large writing desk, the bar contained nothing. It was, in fact, a mere office. Round the counter no thirsty souls pressed to refresh or brutify, as the case might be, themselves. There was not only no drinking but no appearance of drink. The whole thing had very much the appearance of a model temperance house.

Listen! The gong proclaims the dinner hour is at hand. A goodly company sit down, at two large tables arranged parallel with one another in a long room, next above the ground floor. There is abundance of water in these white pitchers; and that waiter-girl is not a little officious in serving it up in these tall-stalked glasses. That jolly-faced gentleman pushes the water from him, as if to obtain more elbow room; at the same time giving a knowing look at those by whom he is more immediately surrounded, the latter replying by a laugh. Consult the bill of fare – 'Turkey, ham, fowl, beef roasted and boiled,' – no wines or liquors, no porter or ale. Model temperance house this; the Vermonters are a law-abiding people.

Pop! Bless me, what is that sound, so strange in such a place? The murder is out at last; and the champagne too. Round it goes. That explains the mysterious knowing look with which the good looking gentleman opposite put away the water from him, as well as the jolly laugh which answered that look.

Let us return from dinner and take a seat in the room, the door of which opens directly upon that dismantled bar. What can be the occupation of that man behind the counter? He seems to have none of the beverages usually found in such places to dispense; and yet he keeps to his post. A little attention suffices to show that in that depth there is deeper still. There is a room behind the bar which is entered by a door at the back of the bar visible – it is the bar invisible to vulgar official eyes. An outward form of compliance with the law has been resorted to in order the more effectually to evade it. The liquor is not publicly exhibited, like stuffed birds in a glass case; but it never fails to come at the magic word of command. It is concealed as much as possible from the outside crowd.

There is some saving of appearances; but if, at dinner, one needs a little stimulant to help digestion, he is not reduced to the necessity of producing a medical certificate: he has only to say to this servant come, and he cometh; and this go, and he goeth. Whatever he demands in the way of beverage is forthcoming.

There is an infinity of private rooms in all large hotels; and to these rooms the law, which aims to prohibit the sale of liquor, has removed the drinking of stimulating beverages. Beyond this it has done little. I saw champagne, brandy, and 'Jeffrey's sparkling Edinburgh ale' go here and there at the word of command, just as if no prohibitory law existed. The sparkling ale, as I can testify, was of prime quality. In reply to an inquiry, I was informed that, during the two years that this law has been in existence, it had not diminished the sale of liquor; the only practical effect was to render liquor more difficult to be obtained by the poorer class who lounge about bar-rooms when liquor is publicly exposed for sale there, but who do not find their way, either to the dinner tables or the private rooms of larger hotels. If the liquor law operates as a restraint in Vermont, at all, it is in this way.

January 21 1856

* * *

An Irish 'poteen' distillery

A correspondent of the *Freeman's Journal*, who has just returned from a tour of considerable extent through the west of Ireland, gives a favourable account of the condition of the inhabitants. He says that even since last year there is a great change for the better, and the signs of improvement are everywhere visible. He attributes this to the abundance of the potato crop, which has led to the re-appearance of the pig, on which animal the Irish peasant mainly depends for the means to pay his rent. At the doors of cabins, where a year ago there was not the sign of a pig, he saw two or three, the other crops were good, but late. It is to be regretted, however, that the people are not content with the legitimate profits of honest and lawful industry. Illicit distillation, notwithstanding the risk involved in it, is carried on to a great extent, and proves highly remunerative, as the manufacturer can realise a handsome profit by selling his whisky at 10s to 14s a gallon, and will always be sure of good customers as long as the present high duty shall be executed.

The principal cereal products of the district are oats and bere,* which are bought in the country markets by private distillers, and carried great distances into the mountains on the backs of ponies to be manufactured into whisky. The following description of a 'poteen' distillery may be interesting, as showing the energy and determination which the peasantry display in the prosecution of this lawless traffic. The writer was conducted to the scene by a friend who was in the confidence of the operators:-

'It lay in a narrow valley between two of the mountains that form the immense chain that runs from the centre of Galway to Westport. Between these mountains runs a rapid stream, ending in a small lake with no visible outlet, and surrounded by granite boulders, which completely stopped all exit from the defile in that direction; in fact, there was only one way to get either in or out. About four miles down the valley, approached by a wretched road, over which no beast of burden could travel except the Western ponies, is a wretched village of some three or four houses, in one of which the still was at full work, and in another the men were grinding malt in the ancient mode between querns. In this house were several barrels filled with fermenting worts. On the side to the mountain was an excavation, the entrance to which seemed to be from behind a large boulder rock, overhung by brushwood, and probably intended as a store for the manufactured goods. Night and day there are sentinels on the mountains that overlook the one narrow road that leads to this extraordinary place; and, if the police were seen coming, a signal could be given, and in 20 minutes three men could consign everything connected with the distillery to the lake, which, they say, is bottomless, and on the arrival of the police not a trace of the work would remain.

The whisky is carried away by night by the members of the family, who have customers for it in different towns and villages. The price is from 10s to 14s per gallon. The people engaged in this illicit traffic certainly make money. There were pigs and poultry about their doors, and flitches of bacon hanging up inside; and one of them had a shop where tea, sugar, bread, and tobacco were sold. On our arrival at the place a man came out and asked in Irish who I was and what brought us there? On a proper explanation we were on the best of terms. We got an excellent breakfast of good strong tea, rashers, eggs, and bread, and, of course, plenty of the 'native' as cream for our tea.'

September 19 1863

BERE – primitive form of barley

* * *

IMPORTANT NOTICE TO THE WINE CONSUMERS OF GREAT BRITAIN

The Cadiz, Oporto, and Light Wine Association (Limited) was originally formed in 1861, to develop Mr Gladstone's new Wine Act. Before that period, in consequence of the heavy duties levied on all wines, it only suited the importer to introduce the higher and more expensive wines of the continent, as, the rate of duty being uniform on the common and highest class wine, it was evident that the merchant, in paying his £34 per pipe duties, would wish to have a proportionate amount of value in his wine, in order to enable him to get his profit and interest of money on his bottled stocks of duty-paid wines.

Thus the foreign wine shippers were only required to send wines of the highest and most expensive character.

It will be seen, upon the slightest consideration of this important question, that this restrictive system of duties was the cause, and only cause, of wines having an artificial value in this country, and not being within the reach of the millions, who in all the other parts of Europe are the principal consumers of the juice of the grape.

In France, Spain, Portugal, Italy, Germany, Hungary, Belgium &c. the peasant and noble enjoy their daily wine, and the same was the case in this country up to the end of the 17th century, when, according to Mr FG Shaw, author of *Wine, the Vine, and the Cellar,* 'the shipments of wines from Bordeaux and Rochelle were enormous even so early as the 14th century, when it appears that upwards of 200 vessels were loaded at Bordeaux for England. In Scotland it was often so abundant that upon the arrival of ships at Leith from Bordeaux casks were placed on wheelbarrows, and the claret sold in the streets in stoupes.'*

The heavy duty of £34 per pipe of 56 dozen effectually put to an end the use of genuine foreign wines by the million, and British compounds and spirituous liquors soon took the place of the generous wines of the continent.

The reduction of the duties by the present Chancellor of the Exchequer, in 1861, has, however, again placed it in the power of the British people to enjoy the light and elegant wines of the most esteemed wine-growing countries of Europe. It is evident that wines of this description can and ought to be purchased in this country as in Paris or Berlin.

January 28 1865

STOUPE – a drinking vessel

* * *

THE ABSINTHE-DRINKER

The *Pall Mall Gazette* has a curious paper on absinthe drinking in France. The writer says:

The indulgence in absinthe which already prevails to great extent among all classes of Frenchmen threatens to become as wide-spread in France and injurious there as opium eating is in China. If a visitor to Paris strolls along the boulevards from the Madelaine to the Bastille some summer's afternoon between five and six o'clock – which is commonly called 'the hour of absinthe' – he can hardly fail to remark hundreds of Parisians seated outside the various cafes or lounging at the counters of the wine shops and imbibing this insidious stimulant. At particular cafes, the Cafe de Bade for example, out of 50 idlers seated at the little round tables 45 will be found thus engaged. But it is not on the boulevards alone that absinthe is the special five o'clock beverage. In most of the wine shops in the faubourgs, in the 'Quartier Latin', and round about the Ecole Militaire, you may see at that particular hour workmen, students, soldiers, clerks, charbonniers, chiffoniers even, mixing their customary draughts of emerald-tinted poison and watching the fantastic movements of the fluid as it sinks to the bottom of the glass, wherein it turns from green to an almost milky white, at the moment when the perfumes of the various aromatic plants from it is distilled disengage themselves.

After the first draught of this poison, which Dr Legrand, who has studied its effects, pronounces to be one of the greatest scourges of our time, you seem to lose your feet, and you mount to a boundless realm without horizon. You probably imagine that you are going in the direction of the infinite, whereas you are simply drifting into the incoherent. Absinthe affects the brain unlike any other stimulant; it produces neither the heavy drunkenness of beer, the furious inebriation of brandy, nor the exhilarant intoxication of wine. It is an ignoble poison, destroying life not until it has more or less brutalised its votaries, and made drivelling idiots of them.

There are two classes of absinthe drinkers. The one, after becoming accustomed to it for a short time, takes to imbibing it in considerable quantities, when all of a sudden delirium declares itself. The other is more regular, and at the same time more moderate in its libations; but upon them the effects, though necessarily more gradual, are none the less sure. Absinthe drinkers of the former class are usually noisy and aggressive during the period of intoxication, which, moreover, lasts much longer than drunkenness produced by spirits of wine, and is followed by extreme depression and a sensation of fatigue which is not to be got rid of. After a while the digestive organs become deranged, the appetite continues to diminish until it is altogether lost, and an intense thirst supplies its place. Now ensues a constant feeling of uneasiness, a painful anxiety, accompanied by sensations of giddiness and tinglings in the ears; and as the day declines hallucinations of sight and hearing begin. A desire of seclusion from friends and acquaintances takes possession of the sufferer, on whose countenance strong marks of disquietude may be seen; his mind is oppressed by a settled melancholy, and his brain affected by a sort of sluggishness which indicates approaching idiocy. During its more active moments he is continually seeing either some imaginary persecutor from whom he is anxious to escape, or the fancied denunciator of some crime he dreams he has committed. From these phantoms he flies to hide himself, or advances passionately towards them protesting his innocence. At this stage the result is certain, and dissolution is rarely delayed very long. The symptom that first causes disquiet to the habitual absinthe drinker is a peculiar affectation of the muscles, commencing with fitful contractions of the lips and muscles of the face and tremblings in the arms, hands and legs. These are presently accompanied by tinglings, numbness, and a distinct loss of physical power; the hair falls off, the countenance becomes wan and sad-looking, the body thin, the skin wrinkled and of a yellowish tinge – everything, in short, indicates marked decline.

Simultaneously with all this lesion of the brain takes place; sleep becomes more and more disturbed by dreams, nightmares, and sudden wakings; ordinary illusions, succeeded by giddiness and headaches, eventually give place to painful hallucinations, to delirium in its most depressing form, hypochondria, and marked impediment of speech. In the end come entire loss of intellect, general paralysis, and death. Paris actually has its clubs of absinthe drinkers, the members of which are pledged to intoxicate themselves with no other stimulant and even drink no other fluid – the only pledges, it is believed, which they do not violate. They assemble daily at some appointed place of rendezvous at a certain hour, and proceed to dissipate their energies and their centimes in draughts of that fatal poison which fills the public and private madhouses of Paris.

These absinthe-drinking clubs are certainly not numerous, but liquor shops abound in all quarters of the city where absinthe may be said to be the staple drink; and lately several have sprung up which, to attract the youth of Paris to them, dispense the insidious beverage at the hands of pretty women.

May 6 1868

CHAPTER TWO

BREWERS UNDER SIEGE

ATTEMPTS to ban barmaids from public houses brought out more than half a million people in protest in 1908, so strong were the feelings about the government's interference in drinking culture. Alcohol, and how far to restrict its sale, was one of the big fault lines in British politics between 1870 and the first world war. The Liberal party, under the control of non-conformist activists, was broadly pro-temperance while the Conservatives favoured the interests of the drinks industry as well as portraying themselves as defenders of the working man's simple pleasures.

By the end of the 19th century, the temperance movement had become a powerful lobbying group in parliament. In 1872 Gladstone's Liberal government introduced a Licensing Act to force pubs to close between midnight and 6am. These mild restrictions led to riots in several towns although the fact that the law didn't apply to clubs where the gentry drank might have had been partly to blame. Gladstone went on to lose the 1874 general election, because, as he saw it, 'We have been borne in a torrent of beer and gin.' However, he was uneasy with hard-line licensing legislation and admitted, 'How can I, who drink … bitter beer every day of my life, coolly stand up and advise hard working fellow creatures to take the pledge?'

By the beginning of the 20th century, the Liberals were still firmly linked to temperance ideas, as was an emerging Labour party, most of whose members were non-drinkers. In fact, many of the early socialists saw temperance reform as an essential element in tackling social problems such as bad housing and chronic ill health. After returning to power with a massive majority, in 1906, the Liberals tried once again to reform the licensing laws. A bill was introduced the following year that would not only have closed a third of all pubs in England but would have banned the employment of women in pubs, thereby killing off that great British institution, the barmaid. Naturally the Conservatives, who by this time had more than 100 MPs with business links to the trade, opposed it, but there was also a massive demonstration against it in London's Hyde Park. While the bill passed the Commons, it was eventually thrown out by the Lords.

Attempts at getting legislation introduced with regard to children and alcohol were rather more successful. In 1886 the sale of drinks to minors under the age of 13 was banned and the Children Act of 1908 made it illegal to administer alcohol to a child under five, except for medicinal purposes, and for under-14s to be in the bars of public houses.

John Edward Taylor, the proprietor of the *Guardian* from 1858 to 1905, and son of the founder, was a firm believer in temperance and wished to see this reflected in the pages of the paper. This was a view broadly shared by his new young editor, CP Scott, who had been appointed in 1872. Certainly, Scott was a man who never completely trusted anyone who he thought drank to excess, but he differed seriously with Taylor on the relative importance of the temperance issue. Letters from Taylor to Scott reiterated that the *Guardian* was not taking a firm enough line. In 1890, he wrote, 'I am sorry you failed to deal with the licensing matter I sent to you…I do not think the MG does its full duty…could you not find a clever fanatic and let him keep all temperance and licensing matters alive?'

Scott though was merely letting a little light into the often stuffy and humourless world of the temperance movement. Amid the lengthy reports of their meetings, there was occasionally a piece that added a touch of colour to the sermons on abstinence. For example, when Francis Murphy, an Irish-born, American temperance evangelist, visited Manchester in February 1882, the paper described in detail his mannerisms and character: 'He has a very considerate command of eloquence, which has been trained and studied more carefully than would at first sight appear, and flavours his utterance with a rollicking Irish humour which is often irresistible. He seems perfectly at home on the platform, laughs at his own jokes, caresses his moustache when he thinks he has said a telling thing, slouches up and down to show how the drunkard slouches home on Saturday night.'

* * *

DRUNKEN CHILDREN

Sir, – On Sunday night last, a little before 11 o'clock, I was passing along Oxford Road, and it was my misfortune to witness a scene which I shall never forget. Between Rusholme Road and All Saints' I came up with a straggling sort of procession consisting of about five lads and about an equal number of girls. One boy appeared to be about 15 years old, and one girl about the same age; all the others would range from about 11 to 14. All of them were intoxicated. One girl especially was so unsteady as to be quite unable to hold up her head, and had she not been supported by two of the biggest boys would have fallen on the ground, and probably have lain there.

Another girl, apparently the youngest, was giving vent to most disgusting language, and threatening in a most dreadful manner what she intended doing to some person, not then present, who had offended her. Being accompanied by my wife and another lady, who were both thoroughly shocked at what they saw and heard, I lost no time in hurrying away. I am not acquainted with the law on the subject, but I think a heavy penalty ought to be inflicted on any publican or beer-seller who would supply drink to young boys or girls. – I am, &c. JA

December 28 1871

* * *

SCENES ON A SATURDAY NIGHT

Sir, – During the last three years I have occasionally made a tour of the principal thoroughfares in the city on Saturday and Sunday nights, for the purpose of learning what was the demeanour of the people in the streets and public-houses &c.

A little after 10 o'clock on a recent Saturday night, passing along London Road, the door of a gin palace was opened by a couple of young women, who were going in. Immediately there broke on the ear a chorus of voices, each talking with great earnestness. Some were arguing, some jesting, some were boasting, some were maudlin. The place was by no means one of the largest of its class, but it contained a mass of persons. Some were mere youths and girls; the majority were young men and women; there were two or three persons who were prematurely old and haggard. The great feature of the mass was poverty. Some were miserably attired; nearly the whole were meanly clad, and many were dirty; some, even amongst the women, were filthy. I am sorry to say that one third of those present were females. There was no actual drunkenness, but nearly all were drink-excited.

Leaving here, I went towards Ancoats. In passing I noticed one or two miserable places – small, wretched beerhouses – evidently, however, not lacking for custom. A little further on stood a large well-built house. Here a cab stopped at the door, from which alighted two young men and young women, going to 'refresh' themselves. The cabman being invited to join them. At the bar stood three or four women and two men. The door was wide ajar. The females appeared not to care for being gazed at by passersby any more than they would had they been in a grocer's shop purchasing sugar or tea. They did not appear to be abandoned women, neither were they of the poorest class; yet they were as unabashed as the men who stood by. I found the same nonchalance manifested by women at nearly all the other spirit vaults and gin palaces I visited. The doors of the greater number were wide open. It seemed to me that I had not previously witnessed anything like the same shamelessness on the part of drinkers and of drink sellers. I certainly thought that I had not before seen so many women drinking openly and unblushingly, and felt that, should further investigation confirm these impressions, few symptoms of moral decadence could be of more serious import. I am sorry to say that nothing I saw subsequently relieved my unpleasant doubts.

Just as 11 o'clock struck I was passing a small street abutting Ancoats Lane. At the corner stands a respectable-looking house; the first door opens into a large bar, the side door leads apparently into the house. A cab had been hailed and a bargain made by a small party of men and women, who then hurried away to the side door of the public house. There was something peculiar about the movements of the party, and I paused for a few moments; it was evident that they were somewhat under the influence of liquor. Presently they reappeared, assisting a respectably-dressed woman, who was helplessly drunk, and utterly insensible to the jokes and disparagements of her companions, some of whom perhaps had drunk no less than she had. It was with difficulty she was hauled into the cab by a man who appeared to be her husband, aided by the others. There was slight vexation at the trouble involved shown by one or two – nothing more serious.

A little later, two miserable women and a mere child came along the Ancoats street; one of the women was considerably the worse for drink, and was partly supported by the other. On the flags just by two men stood talking. Suddenly the most drunken of the two women struck one of the men a back-handed slap in the face. Fortunately the poor fellow was of a patient temper. A bystander fiercely and most unfairly stigmatised him as a coward. He put his hand to his face, and as the vixen seemed inclined to repeat the experiment he moved quietly away. Thus disappointed, she was about to bestow her favours elsewhere, but her stronger and less drunken companion, with the aid of the child, dragged her across the street. A little further I overtook a man and woman. The former looked very angry, the woman was unable to walk steadily, but was evidently trying to persuade him that she was quite sober.

She, poor miserable wretch, seemed conscious that vengeance awaited her, and was anxious to do what she could in order to assuage her husband's wrath.

Here, then, is the history of little more than an hour's observation of the effects of late drinking as seen among females on a Saturday night. I cannot say women, for in more than one case the chief actress was a mere girl. What sort of wives will those girls make? What sort of mothers will they make? Is it to be wondered at that the death-rate in Manchester is disgracefully high, spite of the enormous sums annually spent in sanitary improvements? Is it to be wondered at that children die off rapidly when drunkenness amongst women increases so rapidly? In 1863 there were 799 females apprehended for drunkenness in the city of Manchester, last year there were 2,675; an increase in 10 years of 300 per cent. And be it remembered that the cases apprehended only afford an imperfect index to the real extent of drunkenness which is spreading in our midst.

Something must be done in order at least to stop the increase of this terrible evil. One thing would do much good, and it could be easily effected. Close all places for the sale of liquor at an earlier hour. The change of last year did good, but the good may be greatly augmented. The Legislature has placed the power in the hands of the local magistrates to close public-houses at ten o'clock at night and at nine on Sunday night. The latter limit has been tried in Liverpool, and there are two very strong proofs of the good it has effected. First, the worst class of publicans cry out strongly against it; second, the Sunday night apprehensions of drunkenness have diminished by 284 in the course of less than a year. Let us have the shortest hours the Law permits.

I am, & C.

MD

August 27 1873

* * *

The elections and drinking customs

Sir, – In the many discussions which are taking place on the question of intoxicating drinks it is a matter of wonder that so little reference is made to the practice well-nigh universal in America. Having been in New York during the State elections in November last, I was surprised to find that all hotels and drinking bars were closed during the day of election, at least until the poll was closed. Even after that time, when they were permitted to open, there did not seem to be any great rush for liquor. In point of fact the day was very much like an English Sunday, with the exception that there was no lurking about the public-house door at or near opening times. One of the reasons for this seems to be that drink is nowhere thrust upon you. In England the hotel tables are crowded with glass of every description – for port, for sherry, for claret, for hock, for champagne, and I was about to say for beer – but the tumbler is the hardest to find, lest, perhaps, it might be used for water; but even this is frustrated, for, alas! there is seldom any water to be found, and if any were to be found there would be little temptation to use it, for it is generally stale and not unfrequently tepid. In America there is always a plentiful supply of good clear iced water. Here the wine list is thrust in one's face almost immediately one sits down to the table; there you have to ask for wine if you want it, and the glasses are not brought until the wine is ordered.

Not only is iced water placed ready to your hands in hotels, but at railway stations, in the cars, at theatres, in reading-rooms, and indeed all places of public resort. At all the parks I visited in New York and elsewhere refreshments of all kinds are provided for those who need them, good water being pre-eminently accessible at all times. Lager beer, which is a light and refreshing drink, is a popular beverage with most Americans. This is sold at all the parks. Other liquors are also sold, but they are not thrust upon you as they generally are here.

In all my travels through the States I never saw a single case of drunkenness and I never heard an oath.

I am, & C, An Englishman, Manchester.

March 26 1880

* * *

ADULTERATION OF DRINK
The *Temps*, which has published some alarming facts in regard to the adulteration of the cheaper French wines with logwood and all manner of deleterious substances, has recently turned its attention to beer, with equally disagreeable results. The writer of these articles recounts how, when on a visit to one of the chemists (we do not mean apothecaries) who have aided him in his researches, the heat of the day was oppressive, and some beer was sent for the benefit of the thirsty man of science and the thirsty journalist. The beer arrived, and was poured out – a fine blonde liquor, fresh and sparkling, and altogether delightful

to look at. The journalist was preparing to drink; the chemist, however, declaring that the foam had too much colour in it, insisted on testing the liquid a little first. He took out a little bottle, on which was written 'solution of tannin', and after informing his companion that this solution discoloured genuine beer, he poured a few drops of it into the glass of liquor before him. No change followed; the liquid kept its fine blonde colour unadulterated. The next step was to fetch a little strip of white silk ribbon and steep it in the glass. When he took it out the ribbon had turned yellow. At this the chemist smiled a bitter smile, and informed his journalistic friend that the place of the hops in that beer was taken by pierite acid or extract of bile, and that if they had time to pursue their investigations further they would no doubt find that there was no malt in the beer either.

The malt had doubtless been replaced by glucose, that excellent glucose, of which about 20 million kilogrammes were manufactured in France every year. It is glucose that enables wine to be made without grapes, beer without malt, and cider without apples. It is needless to say that that particular glass of beer was not partaken of.

There remained one thing to be settled, namely, where this very remarkable beer came from. France is hardly responsible, as it manufactures only about one-twentieth of the beer it consumes, the rest coming to it from Austria, England, Belgium, and above all Germany. It appears that Germany is the greatest producer of this detestable compound, and the writer gives an extract from a circular issued by the proprietor of an 'institution for instruction in the manufacture of chemical products,' offering to teach anyone 'how to make beer without hops and without malt' for the very moderate remuneration of 10 shillings. By this process it is declared that 300 per cent can easily be made. Let us hope that no impecunious Englishman may be tempted to turn a dishonest penny out of this new-fashioned kind of brewing.

August 10 1880

* * *

The temperance jubilee

Today the teetotallers of Manchester are, by processions, sports, meetings, and all the recognised formalities of such occasions, to celebrate the 50th anniversary of the 'total' abstinence movement. It is not, of course, intended to imply that there were no water drinkers before Joseph Livesey. In every age there have been individuals who with or without 'pledge' have abstained from intoxicants. There were, it is said, in ancient Egypt persons who were bound by oath not to drink of wine; whilst amongst the Jews there were the Nazarites, Rechabites, and Essenes, sects and communities who were vowed to abstinence. One of the five commandments of the Buddhist is directed against drunkenness, and Mahomet, as is well known, forbade wine to all the true believers – a prohibition which the Wahabees hold to be applicable also to tobacco, for the smoking of which they have invented the phrase of 'drinking the shameful'.

Towards the end of the last and the early part of the present century the intemperate habits of the people appear to have led to organised efforts to mitigate the evil. The first American Temperance Society is said to have been begun in Connecticut in 1789. Gradually the news of this movement reached the old country, but it does not appear that any organised effort was made until 1829, when a Congregational minister of New Ross, Wexford, Ireland, conceived the idea of transplanting the Temperance Society on Irish soil. The progress made at first was not very remarkable, but after a time associations of this kind arose in various parts of Ireland, Scotland, and England. By the middle of 1831 some 30 societies were in existence in England, and 100,000 tracts had been put into circulation. The members were pledged to 'moderation' in use of intoxicants, or at most to abstinence from spirits. The reformers' zeal did not extend to malt liquors, which were still considered innocuous. This was not, however, sufficient for the more ardent and enthusiastic. They began to see the difficulty of defining a hard-and-fast line of moderation. Indeed, as early as 1817 an abstinence society had been formed in Skibbereen, in the county of Cork, and two years later there was at Greenock a Radical Association whose members had likewise pledged themselves to use no intoxicants. But it seems as though they intended this rather as a protest against the high taxation then levied on many articles. There was also the Bible Christian Church in Salford, whose membership was confined to vegetarians and teetotallers. The modern teetotallers, however, date their origin from the 1st September 1832, when, as a result of much discussion in the existing temperance societies, Mr Joseph Livesey and six others signed a pledge 'to abstain from all liquors of an intoxicating quality, whether ale, porter, wine, or ardent spirits, except as medicine'.

It was one of the reformed drunkards of Preston who first applied the word teetotal to express total abstinence from intoxicants. 'Dicky' Turner has been said to be the coiner of the word, but, on the other hand, we are assured that it was a Lancashire provincialism which he merely employed as many had done before him. The term happened to suit the desire of the early advocates for something marking with precision and distinctness their position in relation to what were now called the 'moderation' societies, and hence, for good for evil, the word was adopted by Mr Livesey and his associates.

October 2 1882

* * *

THE BREWERS' EXHIBITION IN LONDON

Considering that beer is still the national beverage and that the public-house is still the club of the majority of the working population, the trade must necessarily assume proportions sufficiently large to justify an Exhibition of its own. Nevertheless the Exhibition in Islington is certainly not what one would like to see it, and what may possibly be seen in the future. Little or nothing in the way of appliance, and the social benefit of the public-house is to be noticed. The prevalent idea seems to be that drinks of all kinds are to be hurled at a customer like so many implements of destruction, and not that he should be allowed to take his ease at his inn and let his heart be glad within him.

At present the publican is not called upon to conduct himself as if he were a benefactor to his species. He is regarded as a man who makes money out of the vices of his fellow creatures. Hence 'Aut bibat aut abeat' is his motto with regard to his customers. Hence, too, a marked contrast between the French cafe and the English public-house with respect to decoration and ornament. In the former all the beautifying is bestowed on the apartment where the customers sit; in the latter on the 'implements of warfare' themselves – the bottles, the beer engines, the spirit casks, the counters, and the shelves lined with plate-glass. Perhaps, however, the sparkle and glitter of a modern publican's bar may be partly due to another reason. The city workman lives in a foggy atmosphere and under a murky sky. The idea of drinking beneath some cool shade, delightful as it might be to Horace, would be simply repulsive to him. As drunkenness is perhaps only one form of the universal desire of the human species to get out of its everyday environments – even by the short and imaginative cut of gin – so it follows that the scene where the English symposium is held should be in marked contrast to the terrible dinginess of ordinary English life – and therefore glittering even to garishness.

The notion of the trade is evidently to mass as much of electro-plate, glass, and reflecting surfaces in the inner side of the bar as possible. The sobriety of aesthetic decoration is almost unknown. In this section Mr Warne, of Blackfriars Road, shows a completely fitted bar, which is certainly handsome enough to rejoice any licensed victualler's heart. One of his specialities is a very neat and ingenious ice safe for producing a constant supply of cold drinking water from the waste of the ice. The growing popularity of lager beer – 'Let's lager' being now a recognised city phrase – is shown by the number of lager beer engines.

Nothing would add to the comfort of barmaids and save the nerves of customers more than a really practical method of opening soda-water bottles without having to draw the cork. Hitherto the united scientific skill of the 19th century has not proved equal to the solution of this mechanical problem, but the idea of Messrs. Codd and Rylands, of Gracechurch Street, seems theoretically sound. The necks of their bottles contain a glass ball which is forced against an India-rubber ring by the aerated water inside, which is thus made to cork itself. A slight tap releases the ball, and the contents then come into your glass or your face, according to your manual dexterity, as is the case of all other soda-water bottles.

From our special correspondent, October 16 1883

* * *

HABITUAL DRUNKARDS ACT

Drunkenness, if it is sometimes a vice, is sometimes a disease. When it is a disease the only effective remedy appears to be total abstinence from intoxicants. This is a remedy that dipsomaniacs are not always ready to adopt. Even when anxious to reform, the drunkard, with his enfeebled moral fibre and pathological craving for stimulants, cannot avoid the numerous occasions that tempt him to excess. For these moral and physical invalids an opportunity of regaining health has been provided in the retreats established under the Habitual Drunkards Act.

No compulsory power is exercised to place a patient within one of these retreats, and in this respect the victim of drink-mania is placed upon a different footing to other 'maniacs'. Whilst this greatly limits the operation of the Act, it cannot be said that our lunacy laws are so successful as to lead to any serious desire for their extension. The number of these retreats for habitual drunkards is six.

The desire of the 'habitual drunkard' to be placed in one of these retreats has to be attended by two magistrates. Limited as the inebriate asylums thus are in operation, the managers generally appear to be convinced by their experience of the good results obtained from this method of treating intemperance. Thus from one retreat comes the declaration:-

'We have increased reason for believing that there are a large number of cases which may be cured by restraint and treatment in retreats, whilst all are benefited for a time.' At one retreat an experiment is being made in receiving habitual drunkards who are unable to pay the full fees, and utilising their services in the garden and farm. The difficulty of finding suitable employment for the enforced leisure of the well-to-do patients is great, but lawn tennis, billiards, gymnasia, workshops, and photographic apparatus help to fill the void. In the winter reliance is also placed upon private theatricals and concerts.

October 26 1886

* * *

DEATH OF THE FIRST 'PLEDGED TEETOTALLER'
The death is announced of Mr John King, 'the first man who signed the teetotal pledge in England', and one of the 'seven men of Preston'. It will be remembered that at the jubilee meeting of the British Temperance League, held

DOUBLE MEASURES

at Exeter Hall in June 1884, there was exhibited the original teetotal pledge signed on the 1st of September, 1832.

The circumstances under which it was drawn up are thus described by the late Mr Joseph Livesey in his, *Reminiscences of Early Teetotalism*:-

'The temperance reformers of the present day have no idea of the conflict that was kept up on this subject. To forbid wine and beer was declared an innovation upon both English and American orthodoxy. I, with many others, felt that there was no safety for our members without this, and we were determined to bring about change. One Thursday (August 23, 1832), John King was passing my shop in Church-street and I invited him in, and after discussing this question, upon which we were both agreed, I asked him if he would sign a pledge of *total* abstinence, to which he consented. I then went to the desk and wrote one out (the precise words of which I don't remember). He came up to the desk, and I said, "Thee sign it first." He did so, and I signed after him. This first step led to the next, for in the course of a few days notice of a special meeting was given, to be held in the Temperance Hall (the Cockpit) the following Saturday night, September 1, at which this subject was warmly discussed. At the close of the meeting I remember well a group of us gathering together, still further debating that matter, which ended in *seven* persons signing a new pledge. The pledge read – 'We agree to abstain from liquors of an intoxicating quality, whether ale, porter, wine, or ardent spirits, except as medicines.'

John King's name appears the last on the list, and he was the only surviving member of the little band. Like Mr Livesey, he was born at Walton-le-Dale, but although associated with the founder of the movement he was not a very prominent advocate of total abstinence, partly through defective education. He hated the drudgery of school life, and shortly before his death he described with much enthusiasm the circumstances under which he left school. He had thrashed the schoolmaster in consequence of being placed too far away from the fire.

January 30 1885

* * *

GIVING BEER TO WORKHOUSE CHILDREN

At the meeting of the Coventry Board of Guardians on Wednesday Mr Loudon referred to the Christmas fare provided for the inmates, and expressed surprise that even little children were served with a portion of beer, the same as the adult inmates. He thought there was nothing more ridiculous than to see children with their heads scarcely reaching above the table drinking beer at dinner. He proposed that beer be not given to children in future – Mr Haywood seconded. Mr Rainbow also expressed his surprise, and added that he supposed it was a survival of an old custom. The Master stated that the allowance to children was the same as to the men – three half-pints during the Christmas season. It was decided unanimously that beer should not in future be supplied to inmates under the age of 16.

January 2 1891

* * *

DANCING WITH ABSINTHE

If there be anyone so fortunately situated that he cannot, when in search of an example of the depths to which drunkenness can drag the most brilliant intellect, find one from his own surroundings, he may welcome a little-known story of De Musset, the French poet, as told by the Danish writer Johan Paulsen, in a collection of *Recollections* which has just been published. As is well known, De Musset, after his rupture with Georges Sand, became a confirmed absinthe drinker, and thus brought about his untimely death. The place in which most of his drinking was done was the Cafe de la Regence. Here he would sit night after night disposing of one glass of absinthe after another. On such occasions the idea of going home never seemed to occur to him, and, if undisturbed, he would remain drinking all through the night and far into the next day. The host and waiters regarded this with much disfavour, but felt at the same time that they could hardly eject so great a poet as if he were an ordinary tippler.

At last a waiter hit upon a way of inducing him to leave of his own free will. He took an enormous glass, filled it brimful with the golden-green stuff, and let water, trickling on to it slowly, turn it to milky white, all in full view of the poet. Then he brought it suddenly close before his face, deftly eluded his attempt to seize it, and backed slowly towards the door. As if compelled by a magnet, De Musset rose from his seat and followed the glass. As soon as he had crossed beyond the threshold the waiter sprang quickly back and closed the door in his face. Next day De Musset had forgotten all about it, or perhaps remembered it only as an alcoholic dream, for night after night the same tragi-comedy was successfully gone through without any subsequent protest on his part.

Miscellany, November 7 1903

ON THE ADVANTAGES OF CLARET

Claret has always been something of a favourite with diet experts, and the current *Lancet* makes a serious effort to bring it into popular favour as a temperate alcoholic beverage. The objection at once arises that good claret is too expensive, even apart from the duty, ever to become a popular substitute for spirits and beer, and that is it better to take pure spirits or beer than bad claret. To this the *Lancet* replies that Bordeaux wines were never cheaper, more abundant, or purer than they are at the present day, and that by far the greater part of the claret sold in this country is sound, natural wine. Samples of claret bought in the open market in London, from wine merchants and grocers, at prices ranging from 1s. to 2s. a bottle, have been tested by the *Lancet*, and the conclusion is reached that 'perfectly good, wholesome, genuine Medoc wine is obtainable at 1s. a bottle'. Even at this price claret is nearly twice as dear as beer. This one might expect from the fact that claret is of nearly twice the alcoholic strength of beer. Notwithstanding this latter circumstance, claret has always been regarded as a 'temperance wine', and it is mainly on this ground that the *Lancet* commends it.

Alcoholic strength is not the only factor. 'The physiological effect of alcohol in claret is in some way checked, and claret is thus less rapidly stimulating than a mixture of spirits and water containing the same proportion of alcohol; in other words, the former is a gentle, while the latter is a rapid stimulant.' The *Lancet* suggests that this may be explained by the presence of other constituents in wine – acids, tannin, glycerine, extractives, and so forth – in a word, to fruit elements. In such a solution the alcohol is less diffusible through animal tissue than in a solution of pure water. If this is so, it is pointed out that the addition of lemon to whisky and water makes it a less harmful stimulant. The *Lancet* thinks that this may be one of the reasons for the decline of claret in popularity, and quotes the ancient dictum that 'you can't get no forrader on it'. More probably it is due to the fact that the growing public that can afford to drink light wines has not acquired the taste for them.

Perhaps a majority of people make their first acquaintance with wine at hotels and restaurants, and it is not encouraging. The men who would be content with a paltry 70 or 100 per cent profit on spirits must have 150 or 200 per cent on wine. Perhaps he thinks that anyone who can afford, permanently or temporary, to order wine at all is fair game. Even then the restaurant claret is usually bad. The *Lancet* admits the existence of spurious claret, and declared that it is sold chiefly by cheap restaurants. On the whole the conclusions of the *Lancet* agree with those of Dr Robert Hutchison, the greatest living authority of diet, who observes that 'sound natural wines are to be obtained at the best economic advantage from the Bordeaux district' and 'the red wines are to be preferred'. If we must take alcohol at all, claret and other natural light wines are probably better for a sedentary population than either beer or spirits. Perhaps the French Government might do something for this national industry by following the example of the Australian State Governments and giving a certificate of genuineness (to be printed on the label of the bottle) to those wines which earn it.

February 7 1906

55

THE 'TRADE'S' DEMONSTRATION

Fourteen processions, 20 platforms, 85 brass bands, 166 special trains from the country to London – such were a few of the arrangements for yesterday's demonstration in Hyde Park against the Licensing Bill. Possibly nothing of the kind has ever had so much money spent on it. The National Trade Defence Association – by what means we are left to conjecture – induced the railway companies to carry the demonstrators for fares which should turn the Final Cup-tie excursionist, let alone the Bank Holiday tripper, green with envy. A bonus was allowed to brewery firms affiliated to the Association who took, for free or other distribution to their employees and dependants, a specially large number of tickets. Under these circumstances many thousands of persons identified with the liquor trade in the various parts of Great Britain enjoyed a very cheap outing in London, where they were welcomed by professional brethren with, of course, unique facilities for entertaining and refreshing them.

It was their duty to attend for a short time at Hyde Park and listen to speeches, but that duty was made very light of them; the Trade Defence Association had considerately limited speech-making to three-quarters of an hour, and on few platforms, apparently, did it last for more than a small fraction of that time. The Sunday crowd, after surveying with interest the bands and banners, seems to have left the orators to their immediate devotees. Money and liquor can buy a good many things, but they cannot buy enthusiasm of the kind which imposes respect. There are in Hyde Park demonstrations, and some of them have claims on the attention of the

Ministry of the day that are beyond challenge; this was not one of them.

Leader, September 28 1908

* * *

THE HOLIDAY AT THE SHOWS

A friend of mine who spent his Whitsuntide in London doing regular London things sends some stray notes of his visits to the White City and Earl's Court. The White City, he writes, is still only partly opened, but so great is the new passion for open-air life among our people that immense crowds were already wandering on Saturday among the empty palaces. Earl's Court is in full swing, and what struck me most about the crowd there on Monday was that it was almost solely a working-class crowd. The middle-class crowd had left London. Never before have I seen Earl's Court handed over to such a democratic crowd. They were an excellent crowd to see. Neither at the White City nor at Earl's Court did I see a single man or woman the worse for drink. The Children Act, I noticed, was having an excellent effect in inducing the family parties to go to the tea-shops instead of the liquor bars. But the crowd was not only sober; it was cheerful and intelligent. I especially noticed the devotion of the parents to their children – a feature that is very much increasing the growing sobriety of the people. Another very pleasing fact is the growing pleasure in music. I do not know whether we Londoners ought to be pleased or sorry at one new feature of our life – the great increase in the number of country visitors. I think we ought to be pleased. There would be some surprising results if a census of origin were taken at some of these exhibitions.

London Correspondence, June 2 1909

* * *

A BABY'S DRINK OF STOUT

Under section 119 of the Children Act, William Clitheroe, loomer, Brownedge, was summoned at Preston yesterday for giving intoxicating liquor to a child under the age of five years.

Warrant Sergeant Williamson said that he saw the defendant, who had a glass of stout in his hand, letting his daughter drink. The child was one year and 11 months old, and was sitting in a bassinette in the doorway of the Wine Lodge. When spoken to the defendant replied, 'I shall let her drink when I think fit.' Beside the bassinette was another girl of eight; the defendant's wife was in the Wine Lodge.

As this was the first case of its kind brought before the Court, the magistrates dealt leniently with the defendant, and fined him 5s and costs.

July 22 1909

* * *

THE CIDER MYTH

A man who was fined at Marylebone for being drunk expressed in the dock his amazement at discovering that cider was not a temperance drink. The belief that 'you can't get drunk on cider' survives in London with the same persistence as the idea that port is non-intoxicating, and with frequently the same unfortunate result. Those who are acquainted with cider-drinking districts know that country folk can, and usually do, consume enormous quantities without evil effect, but the cider sold in the cafes of Brittany or the inns of the Tannus is usually a weak, pleasant, and hardly harmful drink, in comparison with the strong draught cider sold in such London public-houses as sell it at all. Cider is usually drunk in some parts of the country by hard-working people who till the land. In the West of England it is made in October, chiefly by the farmers for themselves and their labourers. It is drunk new, and I believe a gallon a day is considered a fair allowance for a man. Anyone who has sat in a Somersetshire farmhouse opposite a friend with a two-handled brownware quart jar of cider between them knows that it is perhaps the most sociable form of drinking there is. But you cannot live in a cider country without knowing that when a man is drunk in cider he is very drunk indeed, and remains drunk for a long time.

London Correspondence, October 10 1913

CHAPTER THREE
LICENCE TO KILL

UNLIKE 19th-century conflicts, the first world war required citizens to mobilise and help the war effort. Total war demanded an economy geared up to producing huge quantities of weapons and shells, not to mention uniforms and barbed wire. As such, three days after the outbreak of hostilities in August 1914, Herbert Asquith's Liberal government passed the Defence of the Realm Act (DORA), which granted the state extensive powers. These included control of the production and sale of alcoholic drinks, and almost immediately after the Intoxication Liquor (Temporary Restrictions) Act gave magistrates the power to limit opening hours.

During the first few months of the war there was a shortage of weapons, and some believed that drunkenness and absenteeism among the workers were harming armament production and the shipbuilding industry. David Lloyd George, the teetotal chancellor of the exchequer, felt strongly enough to declare, in early 1915, 'We are fighting Germany, Austria and drink; and as far as I can see the greatest of these three deadly foes is drink.'

By May of that year he was munitions minister and setting up the Liquor Control Board. This led to opening hours being cut to five and half hours on weekdays and the introduction of the infamous 'afternoon break' where pubs had to shut for a few hours. Other measures included reducing the strength of beer and banning 'treating', better known as the buying of rounds. There was even talk of the state purchase of the drinks trade and while it was introduced in Carlisle where there was a large concentration of arms factories, it was not expanded to the rest of the country. In fact, much to the annoyance of the temperance movement, some of the state-run pubs became popular among drinkers due to the improved facilities.

The *Guardian*'s editor CP Scott, who had been a Liberal MP from 1895-1906, admired Lloyd George's vigour and fully supported, as he put in a letter to him, his ideal of 'a nation marshalled and regimented for service'. The *Guardian* backed restrictions on drink, at least for the duration of the war, and this was represented in leaders as well as strident pro-temperance comment pieces by Canon Peter Green, the paper's religious contributor, writing under his nom de plume, Artifex.

While full-scale prohibition never occurred in Britain, more successful attempts were being made around the globe. Russia prohibited the consumption of vodka in 1914, an act which some have speculated may have been one of the factors that led to the 1917 revolution, while France banned absinthe in 1915. In the United States, full prohibition was introduced in February 1920, although a number of states had already gone dry. Meanwhile, Australia decided that all pubs had to close by six o'clock. As most workers finished at five this gave exactly one hour to drink, a task they attacked with vigour, giving rise to the quaintly named 'six o'clock swill'. In some states this remained in force into the 1960s.

* * *

THE FINEST SAKE

It is interesting to hear that the Crown Prince of Japan has presented our soldiers in China with a supply of the finest sake. It would be still more interesting to hear what Tommy thinks of it. For an appreciation of the finest sake is a cultivated taste; it is not likely to appeal to any European palate that is not educated up to very dry sherry. Sake is usually described as Japanese beer brewed from rice. It is true that it is brewed from rice as beer is brewed from barley. The process is not that of wine-making, which is the fermentation of the expressed juice. But in spite of the process sake is practically wine. On a sample provided by Mr. Downman, who is the English expert on the subject and, we believe, the only person who ships this exotic beverage to England, one can say that its resemblance to a pale dry sherry in flavour (as well as colour) is quite extraordinary, especially at first tasting. It might almost be mistaken for a light dry manzanilla. Like sherry one can, on analysis of the compound of flavours and aromas, detect beer characteristics, or fancies one can – in particular a peculiar flavour that is characteristic of real Pilsener, which is also brewed from rice. Still, the general fact remains that the Japanese have, to put it roughly, succeeded in making sherry from grain.

Sake classed as a beer is, of course, a very strong one. It is equal in alcoholic strength to a natural unfortified wine. And it is refined and free from sugar, as no European beer is. Japanese do not drink fine sake in wine glasses. They take it in very small porcelain bowls without handles which hold little more than a liqueur glass. It is, in fact, a liqueur rather than a beverage. The sake is heated to bring out the aroma, and is drunk almost as hot as tea. According to the expert, the right way to take sake is with a meal of raw fish – a flaky fish like cod or turbot – and pickled yellow chrysanthemums. But, then, the expert is an enthusiast. He holds that the queer complex of aromas given off by sake is the quintessence of Japan, of delicate woodwork and lacquer, Hokusai and Geishas, and chrysanthemums. However that may be, it is sold in England at about the price of cheap sherry!

On the subject of the beverages of the Allies, a Russian correspondent sends us a further note on vodka. The best vodka, he says, is like any other rye whisky, the bad vodka is just like any bad whisky. The little flasks in which it is brought and from which the Russian peasant deplorably swallows the spirit nest are popularly known as 'little villains'. Now that the vodka is forbidden the Russians will have to restrict themselves to tea and kvass. Kvass is a beverage as blameless as barley-water, made from rye-bread. Russian tea was once pure China. Now it is more often a blend of China tea with the other teas of the Indies. But is still a smoother-flavoured, blander beverage than the 'rough' teas that are most popular here.

Miscellany, October 22 1914

* * *

WAR AND STRONG SPIRITS

At the beginning of the war vodka, the national spirit of Russia, was prohibited in Russia, and absinthe, the pernicious decoction of wormwood so popular in France, and similar liquors, temporarily, in France. President Poincare has now extended the prohibition by decree until a Bill can be passed through Parliament in the coming session which will make it permanent. If we reflect how far we are in this country from any prohibition of spirit-drinking, and – to be candid – how unthinkable such a step is to the average man, we shall get an idea of the seriousness with which France is facing her task and the intensity of the 'will to conquer' which she shows. It is true, no doubt, that the ravages of vodka and absinthe are worse than those of the spirits consumed in this country, but the difference between our attitude and that of France and Russia is due rather to the intensity with which they are forced to realise the war. We can do our utmost to imagine what war and invasion mean, but we have only the imagination to help us; they have the real thing burning in their consciousness, the necessity of straining every sinew to put an end to it. Vodka and absinthe are a hindrance to success in war. Therefore they are abolished. And is not spirit drinking also, as practised here, a hindrance, even in a less degree? There is another question, too. How is it that a nation does for the purposes of war what it does not think necessary for the national lifetime of peace?

Leader, January 1 1915

* * *

The war and temperance

Ought any further temperance measures to be taken in view of the war, and, if so, what? It is a question which we ought to be able to discuss without reviving old and party controversies. Those who have always been in favour of great restrictions on the sale of liquor or of complete prohibition will continue to hold their views for their old reasons, and so will their immemorial opponents. But the war has put a new face on things. The world is not the same for anyone – for anyone, at least, with an imagination or a conscience – that it was last July. All our stock problems stand in a different light, for in working at them nowadays we are consciously aiming at a definite, clear-cut end in an immense enterprise which the war has thrown across the national life. The Premier spoke some time since of the 'terrible and unspeakable possibilities' with which the nation has to reckon, and although our isolation prevents us from realising like a Belgian or a Frenchman the horror and magnitude of the struggle in which we are involved, we are all agreed that if duty and performance went hand in hand we should be putting every ounce of energy, both as a community and as individuals, into the one great task. This task we define as 'ending the war' or 'seeing it through' – rough practical phrases which conceal the truth that what we are now fighting for is our national life and the right to hand on the principles and the liberties on which it hangs. Just because this has been realised, there have been general manifestations of the desire to 'do something'. To render some service, however small, to the common cause. And just because of the need of concentrating all the powers of the nation in one direction there are many who think we are dealing too carelessly with the liquor question. Is it worthy of us, they say, at such a crisis to allow the sale and distribution of liquor to continue with such trifling restrictions as have been put in force? If we were really patriots, lovers of our country, should we not deal more severely with a habit which it is agreed may be and often is injurious to efficiency and health, and if general restriction is impossible without some slight self-sacrifice on the part of a large section of the population, is there anyone who would refuse it if he had once recognised that his personal sacrifice meant the public good? 'It is a sweet and seemly thing,' says the tag, 'to die for one's country.' But for those who cannot die in a trench it is not enough to repeat an honoured tag. The question is what they can do at home to serve the same end.

We know what other nations have done, and we should not be deterred from realising the meaning of their action by those who say that Russia and France are different from England, or that vodka and absinthe are more damaging to mind and body than our strong spirits. In fact, the restrictions in France extend far beyond absinthe, and in Russia the local authorities in all parts of the country have been asking and obtaining permission to close wine shops and saloons. Nor does it matter whether British spirits are more or less injurious than others; the only question that concerns us is whether they are liable to be so used or abused as to hinder us in the successful prosecution of our task. So far as the soldiers are concerned, the answer is not doubtful, and it is difficult to understand how anyone can be satisfied with the present state of things. No soldier does his work the better for drink; if he is to do it with the maximum of bodily efficiency and mental alertness, the less liquor he has the better. Yet we still permit soldiers on leave to be served by the trade and treated by the kindness of their friends; how much of it goes on everyone knows who uses his eyes, though few cases may figure in the courts. These men, in their own interests and that of the work they have to do, should be saved from all such 'kindness', and a proper system of penalties should apply to those who, from whatever motive, sought to ignore or evade a prohibitory order. That the soldiers themselves would be seriously discontented we do not for a moment believe; the men who have gone through the campaign or have offered themselves with their eyes open to share its hardships are not the stuff to complain more loudly or more seriously than the British soldier knows he is, on all occasions, privileged to do. After all, he would be no worse off than if he were a policeman. But in any event, what we ought to consider is simply whether the efficiency of the army machine – the striking arm on which we depend on land – does not stand to be increased, whether substantially or not, by prohibiting the public sale and distribution of strong drink to all soldiers for the period of war. Some may say, 'Yes, but after all it is a small matter.' There are no small matters at such a time as this.

Still, the men who fight are only part of the problem. There is the mass of the population also, and with it comes the question whether there should not be at least a considerable restriction of hours. Some will say, 'Prohibition for the army by all means, but why worry the countless crowd of those who will never have to fight?' It would be quite reasonable to argue that if alcohol lowers the efficiency of a soldier it must have a similar effect on the man who is engaged on any work which demands a steady hand, a quick eye, or clear head. Those who admit the argument for debarring a soldier from supplies of liquor, but would place no restrictions in the way of the skilled manual labourer or the brain-worker, stand on dangerous ground if they grant the premise that all of us must put our best into the common stock. It is all a question of how seriously we take ourselves and the national emergency. Nothing effectual can be done without a real movement of public opinion, the real readiness and desire to save our strength and our money for the service of the nation in its time of trial. This is what has given its force and value to the movement for restriction in the other great countries which are fighting side by side with us in the war. Drink in excess is an injury and a loss not only to the individual but to the nation; drink in any case is an indulgence to be restricted like other indulgences when all our resources are needed for a great common effort. There is no question here of Puritanism or of a desire on the part of one set of men to impose their own views upon others who do not share them. We live in a time of national peril, when a great emergency has to be faced with all the energy alike of our soldiers and of our industrial population. We are in a sense all soldiers; we ought to be sparing of our pleasures and lavish of our services. One easy way of doing our duty in this way is to follow, though it be at a distance, the splendid example of Russia and of France and to give to our country the strength and the resources which we are too apt to waste.

Leader, February 27 1915

* * *

TEMPERANCE IS RELATIVE
In one respect total prohibition might produce some curious confusions, for as time has gone on different counties and districts have formed their own ideas as to what is and what is not alcoholic liquor, and those ideas would not be likely to agree with the decision of the

authorities. In Lancashire and Cheshire, for instance, there are many people, especially women, who do not regard port (or port-wine in the more precise local speech) as alcoholic, and it is quite common to hear of it as a temperance drink. Possibly this arises from the custom in the North of having a decanter of port as one of the attractions of a confectioner's shop. There are other parts of the country where beer, especially home-brewed beer, is considered to be on the 'water waggon' list.

A great many people regard cider as exempt, but old cider may be a most potent liquor, and one can remember seeing the village worthies of a Norfolk hamlet returning home in strange and devious ways after celebrating the birthday of the local publican by (quite innocently) drinking his health in some very special old cider. A glass of cherry brandy on a cold day would involve no pledge-breaking in the eyes of some worthy people one has known. And who has attended an old-fashioned funeral, with its 'sherry-wine' and its cake, without seeing people toss off their glass with an unruffled assurance of teetotalism? On the other hand, it is very well known that there are temperance drinks containing quite an appreciable quantity of alcohol, while as for the much fermented home-made wines made from various garden products, some of them attain of a potency positively dangerous.

Miscellany, April 7 1915

* * *

EFFECT OF NO TREATING
London has begun life under the no-treating order today with characteristic resignation. All the same, the order is

highly unpopular. The immediate effect has been a big drop in the takings at every public house. I am told that the decrease of 25 per cent was common in the ordinary London bar today. In Scotland under the no-treating system I learn, on best authority, that the decrease in takings ranged from 25 per cent to 40 per cent.

An incident described by a publican today was probably repeated in most London bars many times. The publican said:- 'There are three customers who always come in about luncheon-time, and each of them stands a drink, making nine drinks in all. Today they came in as usual. They each ordered one drink. Then one of them, still feeling dry, ordered another, but the others did not think it was up to them to do the same. The result was – four drinks instead of nine.'

The effect of the licensed trade will undoubtedly be severe, as London is a place of much business entertainment. At a luncheon counter in one of the more expensive places men were handing one another the bill of fare and saying, 'What will you have?' Then a drink, of course, went with the food. But that sort of thing is too expensive to last. The great fact is that the pace of drinking has visibly slackened, and that many who went into taverns today to experience the novelty of treating themselves will become only rare visitors. The really important effect on the individual will be that a man will now realise how much his drinking costs him, for he will no longer be able to deceive himself with the belief that he was entertaining others.

What is a meal?

The public-house keepers here are taking no risks, and some are even refusing to allow a man to pay for his friend's ginger-beer. The usual rule, however, is to allow the orderer of a bottle of soda-water to pour part of it into his friend's whisky. On the great question as to what is a meal, the general view with publicans is that nothing short of a plate of meat and vegetables is a legal meal. The say that bread and cheese might well be a meal, but that brings in the plate of sandwiches question, so it is much simpler to make it something that is beyond quibble. A few of them, however, allow treating with bread and cheese. Ingenious persons were going about today citing all sorts of conundrums to the worried licensees, such as the man who brought his dinner with him and asked whether he could treat his friends while he ate it at the bar.

The suppression of treating is likely to lead to the disuse of the convivial sort of gathering – smoking concerts and so on – at which it is usual for a host to entertain a 'table' of guests. An old English custom will now pass, much to the relief of the hero of it. The host of the suburban inn or the distillery traveller will no longer entertain 'the bar' for the 'good of the house'.

October 12 1915

* * *

RUSSIA WITHOUT VODKA

For years drink has been the besetting crippling sin of the Russian people. For the last four hundred years vodka has affected every page of their history. And now by one of the greatest reforms in the history of the world – great because it has achieved the greatest results in the shortest time – a nation of 150,000,000 souls has passed as it were in a night from the empire of vodka into the empire of light.

It is, perhaps, hard for the English people to realise the importance of this measure. There has been much talk of the £80,000,000 or £90,000,000 sterling which Russia derives annually from her drink bill, but when all is said and done this sum, if spread over the whole population, shows that Russia spends less on drink per head than almost any other European people. The point of interest is not in the amount of money expended, but in the amount of strong spirit which is consumed. Of Russia's total drink bill more than 40 per cent is spent on vodka.

At the present moment the position in Russia as regards alcoholic drinks amounts practically to total prohibition. When the mobilisation was ordered the Government spirit shops (the sale of vodka is a Government monopoly) were closed. They have remained closed ever since, and the Emperor has promised that the Government sale of vodka shall never be resumed. This, however, is not all. In nearly all the large towns of Russia there is a total prohibition of alcoholic drinks of even the mildest sort, and in Moscow, for instance, it is impossible to procure in a legitimate manner even a bottle of red wine without a doctor's certificate!

How has this affected the Russian people and how has it affected the war? We are told on the best authority – that is, by the Germans themselves – that the chief factor in the upsetting of German calculations was the unexpectedly rapid mobilisation of the Russian forces. Those who remember the mobilisation days during the Japanese War will know what the absence of vodka meant to the mobilisation of 1914. 'If vodka had not been forbidden,' writes a peasant to the *Russkiva Viedomosti*, one of the most serious Russian newspapers, 'our village would have suffered complete ruin. Every man taken for the mobilisation would have spent at least 10 roubles on this worthless drink. In our village 32 men were taken. In this way 320 roubles would have been spent on vodka. Besides this, the relatives of those taken would have spent from two to three roubles 'to drown their sorrows'. They would not have stopped to consider that they were ruining themselves, but would have sold their last sheep in order to celebrate the occasion. In this way not less that 800 roubles would have been thrown away. This is an enormous sum of money for our village. And then, too, how much brawling, fighting, quarrelling, and even murder there was have been! Apply this test to every village and town in Russia and add to it the fact that with the drunkenness it would have been impossible to bring the men to the mobilisation points, and the result shows the difference between a mobilisation with vodka and a mobilisation without it.'

Certain statistics are already available regarding the effect of abstinence from vodka on the internal life of the country. These statistics show very remarkable results even when one makes due allowance for the normal conditions which have been created by the calling out of a large part of the male population to the war. The first most striking feature is the decrease of crime and hooliganism which is reported from every corner of the Russian Empire.

Still more striking is the decrease in sickness among the factory workpeople and the consequent increase in efficiency. In Russia the one-day illness is one of the banes of the factory manager's life. After every holiday it is an exception if more than one-half of the male workers put in an appearance on the following day. Today, however, with the cessation of the sale of vodka the after holiday illness has disappeared.

From a correspondent, March 10 1915

* * *

DRINK RESTRICTION ORDER: ALL PUBLIC HOUSES IN THE WESTERN COMMAND

The military authorities have issued an order restricting the hours within which intoxicating drink may be sold in licensed houses in an area covering Wales, the counties of Chester, Hereford, Monmouth, Lancaster, Cumberland, Westmorland, and the Isle of Man, and designated by the War Office the Western Command. The order is in the following terms:-

In compliance with a direction received from Field Marshal the Right Hon. Earl Kitchener of Kartoum, K.P, G.C.B., &c., the General Officer Commanding-in-Chief of the Western Command has made an order under Regulation 10 of the Defence of the Realm (consolidation) Regulations Act, 1914, directing that on and after Monday next, the 29th inst., all licensed premises (whether for consumption on or off the premises) shall only be opened during the undermentioned hours:-

Weekdays between the hours of 10.30am and 10pm. Sundays between the hours 12.30pm. and 2.30pm and between the hours 6.30pm and 9pm.

Regulation 10 provides that 'the competent naval or military authority may by order require all or any premises licensed for the sale of intoxicating liquor within any area specified in the order to be closed, except during such hours and for such purposes as may be specified in the order either generally or as respects the members of any of his Majesty's forces mentioned in the order, and if the holder of the licence in respect of any such premises fails to comply with the order he shall be guilty of an offence under these regulations, and the competent naval or military authority may cause such steps to be taken as may be necessary to enforce compliance with the order.'

March 26 1915

* * *

THE EARLIER CLOSING ORDER

A section of the Defence of the Realm Act gives the competent military authorities power to curtail the hours during which licensed premises may legally be open. General Sir Henry Mackinnon, acting under instructions from Lord Kitchener, yesterday used his powers under this section and issued an Order closing licensed premises except between 10.30 in the morning and ten in the evening. This Order is to come into force on Monday next over the whole of the Western Command, a large district extending from South Wales to the borders of Scotland. The restriction in the hours of sale in not a very serious one, and we imagine that it will be criticised not for doing so much but for doing so little. The knocking off a couple of hours or so in the morning and an hour at night may reduce the abuse of alcohol to some slight extent, and to that extent increase our national efficiency for war, but is somewhat of an anticlimax after all that has been written and said in praise of sobriety as a special national duty at this time. Mr Lloyd George at Bangor said that intemperance was hurting the country more than all the German submarines, and if that be so and we were really in earnest about the war and about the ill-effects of alcohol on national efficiency we should no more be satisfied with three hours' reduction every day in the ravages of alcohol than with a three hours' close time every day for the enemy's submarines. We believe that the public would support restrictions much more considerable than are now imposed. It is one thing, however, for the people to impose restrictions on themselves; it is another and much more difficult thing to impose restrictions on the people. There are no limits that the people could and would do in this matter by their own act; but the military authorities, through nominally omnipotent and backed by all the prestige of a great war, are apt to move warily for fear of not being supported by public opinion. It is a pity that there is no provision in our Constitution for voluntary action by the people themselves.

The section of the Defence of the Realm Act under which yesterday's Order was made does not, as we read it, apply to clubs. We quote the words of the section in another column, and it would seem to be clear that clubs are not licensed premises within the Act. There is, however, another Act which became law on August 31 last which gives justices power to suspend the supply of liquor both in licensed houses and in clubs. Two conditions are attached by the Act to the exercise of this power. First, the chief officer of police must recommend that restrictions are desirable 'for the maintenance of order of the suppression of drunkenness.' The second condition makes the consent of the Home Secretary necessary to any order under this Act for closing before nine o'clock. Some chief constables (among them apparently the Chief Constable of Manchester) interpret the works of the Act as meaning that these powers should not be exercised unless there has been an actual increase of disorder or of drunkenness before the war, or at any rate some reason to apprehend it. On this view the amount of disorder and drunkenness before the war is to be taken as a permissible norm which must be transgressed before any action is taken. That view leaves entirely out of account the necessity which the war has put on the country of screwing up its standard of conduct and efficiency. Another view, broader and more rational, is that taken by the Birmingham justices yesterday, which holds that magistrates have full discretionary powers which it is their duty to interpret after taking all the facts into account, and among them the tremendous fact of the war and of the duty of screwing up our national efficiency by every legitimate means. But, whatever ground there was for two opinions on the meaning of the Act before the issue of the military Order of yesterday, there can be no doubt about the duty of the magistrates now. They must enforce on clubs the same restrictions as the military Order imposes on licensed houses. Not to do so would be unfair to licence-holders and impose on them and on their customers a higher standard of patriotic sacrifice than on the managers and members of clubs. What is more, it would go far to defeat the objects of yesterday's Order. Licensing justices will either be loyal to yesterday's Order or they will not.

If they are loyal they will extend the Order (with only such modifications as may be strictly necessary) to clubs. If they fail to do that they will be doing their best to defeat the military policy of the country.

One criticism may be made on the form of yesterday's Order. The Act gives the military authorities very wide discretion. Licensed premises may, in the words of the Act, be closed 'except during such hours and for such purposes' as may be specified by the Order. The words seem to give the military authorities power to prohibit the sale of intoxicating liquors in the licensed houses without actually closing their doors. We are inclined to regret that this discretion was not used, while at the same time the restrictions on the sale of intoxicants were made more stringent, for there are very many poor people whose only chance of seeing company on most days of the week is in the public-house. There is no gain in shutting down such social life as the public house may provide, so long as there is no sale of intoxicating drink, and it might lead to some wholesome changes in the life of the people if the public-house were encouraged to be a public-house in the real sense and not a mere drinking shop. It may not be too late even now to revise the form of yesterday's Order in this sense. Magistrates under the Act of August last have a less wide discretion. They may under the Act suspend the supply of intoxicating liquor in clubs, but they have no power to close the clubs. It is desirable that as regards the supply of intoxicating liquor clubs and licensed houses should be put on the same footing, and as clubs cannot be closed it might be reasonable to give licensed houses the right to keep open during the hours for which they are ordinarily licensed so long as they do not supply intoxicating liquor.

March 26 1915

* * *

NIGHT-CLUB DODGES

Some recent cases in courts-martial and in the criminal courts have informed the authorities about what was common gossip in town – namely, the almost undisguised drinking and other evasions of the law in some night clubs. New and stringent regulations about these resorts will be made very soon. Drink, and extremely bad drink, is known to be easily obtained at four places within a policeman's beat of Leicester Square. The homage vice paid to virtue was that a lemonade bottle was placed in front of each drinker of whisky and soda. But at the best night clubs there is really no intoxicating liquor, although the members and 'visitors' are led to believe quite the contrary. At one famous club, recently closed, they sold 'champagnette', which in reality was a preparation of apple-juice carbonised by an aerating machine, and really certified as a temperance drink. At other clubs the great thing is the 'cup'. It is the same preparation with something added to give it a 'bite'. The 'bite' is usually tincture of capsicums.

In one of two clubs under the special attention of the Provost Marshal's staff nobody is, of course, ever seen in uniform, but I have been told that to prevent the inconvenience of not being able to be present the management have a supply of mufti into which officers can change on arriving, changing their clothes again on leaving. I should like to see a caricaturist's picture of, say, the 'Ten Thousand Club' with half the dancers in these hand-me-down-outfits and the Provost Marshal standing by still unable to spot his prey. The 'Ten Thousand Club' is the name given for a night club in the new play 'The Only Girl'. The valet explains to some wives who are looking for their husbands that it was given because ten thousand is the number of its honorary members.

September 28 1915

* * *

NON-ALCOHOLIC BEER

Much has been heard lately of the virtues of the officially-recommended non-alcoholic beer and its growing popularity. These reports – and the hot weather – have sent many people in search of it to the licensed houses. After a pilgrimage today a tavern was discovered in the newspaper area where 'Government beer' was to be had. It resembled a dark lager that has been drawn some time – a harmless, thirst-quenching drink. The popular notion that non-alcoholic beer is actually made under the supervision of the Central Liquor Control Board is a delusion. Various kinds of non-alcoholic beer are supplied, together with alcoholic beers, to the munition canteens, and they are said to be quite popular in spite of the inevitable absence of 'body'. These beers all come within the legal definition; that is they do not contain more than two per cent proof spirit and do not exceed 1.016 specific gravity.

May 25 1916

'GRETNA TAVERN': FIRST EXPERIMENT IN STATE CONTROL

The Gretna Tavern, at Carlisle, which was opened by Lord Lonsdale this afternoon, is the first of the 'reformed' public-houses which are to be provided by the Liquor Control Board under the State purchase scheme in the Carlisle and Annan district. When the Board decided to take over the Carlisle licensed premises a few weeks ago their attention was first directed to measures to reduce the congestion at drinking bars caused by the incursion of thousands of labourers and navvies into the city. The old Post Office building was placed at their disposal, and within a month it has been refitted and decorated for use as a tavern where the Gretna workers may obtain food and non-intoxicant drinks as well as alcoholic liquor.

A 'tavern' on new lines

The contrast between the Gretna Tavern and the ordinary public-house, apart from its comprehensive equipment as a victualling-house, is found in the extent and loftiness of the rooms. The entrance door opens on to a wide passage, and immediately to the right of this is the bar, which was formerly the public business-room of the Post Office. A long counter runs down this room, and behind it are ranged barrels of beer and stout, with many boxes of mineral waters. The space for customers in front of the counter is 10 or 12 feet wide, and one would estimate that a hundred or more men can be served here without overcrowding. A few chairs stand in a row against the wall, but the intention is that the bar shall be mainly used as a stand-up drinking place. The spaciousness of the room will enable the waiters to maintain effective supervision without much difficulty.

The part of the building which justifies the use of the word 'tavern' in its old English sense is at the end of the passage. Here is a large room with white walls rising above a deep skirting of dark oilcloth to a high vaulted roof with skylights. It used to be the sorting-room of the Post Office, and little alteration was needed, apart from the simple decoration and the covering of the floor with dark green cork linoleum. Heavy tables of unstained wood of good design and finish, covered with thick white linoleum, are placed in three rows down the room, and each of the dark-stained chairs bears the monogram in green letters 'G.R.I.' under a crown. There is sufficient accommodation at the tables for at least a hundred persons, and many others will be able to sit in various spaces about the room.

Extending across nearly the whole of one end is a buffet stand filled with various kinds of fruit and cakes, a stack of small loaves, hard-boiled eggs, sandwiches, chocolates, tobaccos and cigarettes, all attractively displayed. Neat little posters on the walls set forth the tariff, and the list opens with non-intoxicating refreshments. Tea is a penny a cup, and milk a penny a glass. Draught ale and stout are twopence a half-pint and threepence-halfpenny a pint. Bottles are twopence-halfpenny. Barley-water is to be sold at a penny a glass, and it will be interesting to learn if the thirst-quenching virtues of this drink are appreciated by the navvies. No spirits or wines are to be sold in the building, but other intoxicants will be supplied in the tavern either with or without food. In one corner of the room is a small newspaper stand, and a piano and gramophone are provided for the entertainment of the men.

July 13 1916

* * *

NEW BOOKS: *NOTES ON A CELLAR BOOK* BY GEORGE SAINTSBURY

'There is absolutely no scientific proof of a trustworthy kind,' says Professor Saintsbury, discharging a howitzer early in the affair, 'that moderate consumption of sound alcoholic liquor does a healthy body any harm at all; while on the other hand there is the unbroken testimony of all history that alcoholic liquors have been used by the strongest, wisest, handsomest, and in every way best races of all time…'; and a little later he adds: 'It is sometimes forgotten that only one of the two peaks of Parnassus was sacred to Apollo, the other belonging to Dionysus. The present writer has spent much of his life in doing his best, as he could not produce things worthy of Phoebus, to celebrate and expound them. It cannot be altogether unfitting that he should, before dropping the pen altogether, pay such literary respects as he may to the other sovereign of the 'duplicate horn'. The framework of this tribute to Bacchus is the notes the author has kept of the contents of a small but carefully-chosen cellar founded in 1878. It was replenished and expanded more or less devoutly through periods at Oxford, at Guernsey, at Elgin, and at Edinburgh. While in Manchester he had 'neither time nor means to invest in the gifts of Bacchus', and indeed, had no good to say of the place at all except that in the old Palatine Restaurant they used hock bottles as water carafes. It was evidently a cellar distinguished as much by catholicity of taste as by care in buying, for, small though it was, it seems to have contained samples of most known liquors, from the Hermitage of '46 'whose brown was flooded with such a sanguine as altogether transfigured it, whose bouquet was like that of the less sweet wall-flowers, and over whose flavour one might easily go into dithyrambs,' to the cask of beer which reached him up the Thames, 'affectionately labelled "Mr George Saintsbury. Full to the bung." I detached the card,' says the author, 'and I believe I have it to this day, as my choicest, because quite unsolicited, testimonial.' He is, one detects, as sound and immovable a conservative in the choice of his wines as in all else, inclining in his allegiance to claret, burgundy, or port. Of the last he says, differing from Mr. George Meredith, that those who have 40 year old port in their cellars 'had best drink it.' But experience in Elgin and in Edinburgh has made him not less a connoisseur of whisky, and he has a good word to say even for the discredited gin, whose latter-day obloquy he dismisses with the splendidly illogical contention that there is no more real reason for it than there is for abusing water because the Inquisitors employed the water torture. Indeed, the attitude towards all liquors which Professor Saintsbury preserves in this rich treasury of lore and wisdom concerning them is that of the fabled Scotchman who remarked that while no doubt there was good whisky and better whisky there was no such thing as bad whisky.

ASW, August 9 1920

CHAPTER FOUR

BEHIND CLOSED DOORS

IF drinkers and the brewing industry thought that the end of hostilities in 1918 would restore things to their pre-war state, they were very much mistaken. The 1921 Licensing Act was to consolidate many of the temporary measures of the war years such as shorter licensing hours and weaker drink. In fact a number of these would remain in place for much of the rest of the century. However, the first world war saw the high point of the temperance movement – in 1916 a petition calling for prohibition attracted 2.5 million signatures – and after that the movement's influence gradually waned.

While the act restricted drinking to nine hours in the capital and eight elsewhere, clubs were free to do what they wanted, particularly with regard to afternoon and Sunday drinking. Upper-middle-class clubs had been around for more than one hundred years but working men's ones had started to appear in the 1860s, initially as teetotal alternatives to pubs. The members though soon exploited the rules that had been set up for gentlemen's clubs and began to sell and brew their own beer. After the war the clubs really took off, often with their own breweries, and by 1924 there were 2,500 of them in England and Wales.

As for nightclubs, these were supposed to stop serving drink at the same time as pubs. However, they sprang up in response to the early closing restrictions, and the 1920s saw them often being raided, as sensationally reported in the Sunday newspapers. In response, private 'bottle parties' began to be held which, in theory, were beyond the jurisdiction of the authorities. The 1920s was the era of the cocktail party, at least in London. These had been around for a few years – Arthur Ransome, later to be the *Guardian*'s Russia correspondent, wrote about an American girl making an Opal Hush* in his 1907 book *Bohemia in London* – but cocktail parties became all the rage after the introduction of prohibition in the US. Concoctions were invented to make illicit drinks look innocent or disguise rough alcohol. Rich Americans came over to England and the bright young things partied.

However, by the end of the decade the sheen was beginning to wear off and Evelyn Waugh was writing dismissively of 'cocktail parties given in basement flats by spotty announcers at the BBC'. Perhaps reflecting the mood of the times, cocktail parties gradually began to be replaced by sherry parties during the 1930s.

Away from the rarefied air of these gatherings, the bulk of the population was still drinking beer, although consumption was decreasing. Brewers were having to think of new ways of attracting customers, and beer in cans began to appear in 1930, although this did not really catch on. Bottled beer was more successful and gradually gained a foothold in the market. New types of pub began to be built too, especially in the recently developed suburbs, and at road intersections to cater for the growth in private motoring. These had gardens, provided entertainment, food and even women's toilets. They were often built in a mock-Tudor style, and John Betjeman referred to them in Slough, his 1937 poem where he wrote of 'bald young clerks' going to Maidenhead, 'And talk of sport and makes of cars/In various bogus-Tudor bars.' Not all were successful but they did improve the image of the pub, becoming less threatening, particularly for women.

* OPAL HUSH – *one part claret; three parts chilled lemonade*

MANCHESTER'S DRUNKENNESS CHART

Some striking but easily intelligible variations in the amount of Manchester drunkenness during 1919 and 1920 are recorded elsewhere in a report from the Chief Constable. During the war, for well-known reasons, drunkenness greatly decreased. The year 1919 and the early part of 1920 were periods of military demobilisation. Some millions of young men and of women war-workers were thrown idle, at any rate for a little time, with a little money in their pockets. In every camp or barracks the amount of drinking rushes up, as a matter of course, on the evening after a pay parade and on the next day; and England during 1919 was the scene of the most enormous pay parade in her history. It was also a year of high wages – of dear beer too, no doubt, but, in the cotton and woollen districts, of wages more than proportionately good. This is not to say that there is any necessary connection between good wages and drunkenness. It is simply a fact of present experience that if a man likes beer he usually buys more of it, as he does of other things, when he has more money to spare.

Of course it was not to be hoped that men would come back from active service more abstemious than they went to it. Their life in the field, whatever else it was too, was generally dreary, monotonous, and trying to nerves – all conditions predisposing men to drink; beer remained cheap in canteens overseas when it had become dear at home; there was often little or nothing else for a man to spend his pay upon; in a good many places there was no warmed and lighted room for men to sit and talk in except a French or Belgian village alehouse; and, though there were the punishments of a felony for drunkenness on duty, authority – perhaps partly for that very reason – was at other times inclined to be lenient to anything not too flagrant to be overlooked. The idea that either military discipline or the mental exaltation of combatant service tends to make teetotallers is, of course, only a sentimental dream. Manchester has now received back her portion of the demobilised host, and the process has left her with a monthly tale of charges of drunkenness. Our measure of consolation is that, at its highest, it is far lower than the pre-war rate. We have no sure means of distributing the credit for this improvement as between the general and permanent tendency of the country to work drunkenness out of its system and the special obstacles which the war has placed in the way of heavy drinking – the high cost of drink and the reduced hours of sale. The latter have certainly counted for something at any rate. It is idle to say, as is often done, that the State cannot, in any degree, 'make people sober by Act of Parliament'. It certainly cannot instantly change the heart, but in some degree or other not only the State, experience shows, can make men sober, but every licensing bench which withholds an extra drinking facility does it. The man who gets drunk is usually not a person of iron resolution unflinchingly pursuing his beloved object through every difficulty that man may make for him. He is more like a sheep that will not break down a fence to get at clover, but will eat it till she dies of flatulency if you leave the gate open opposite her muzzle.

Leader, January 5 1921

* * *

THE DECLINE OF THE WINE CELLAR

The absence of wine cellars in some new town houses in London has led to many reflections on the change that has come over wine drinking in London. Is the habit of drinking wine going the same way as the old observances of taking 'a glass of wine with you, sir', and of the men settling down after dinner and sending the port round and round? Undoubtedly there is much less wine drunk, especially clarets and burgundies. Whisky and soda or light wines or cider are the usual luncheon drinks at the clubs, and at dinner for those who can afford it champagne is becoming almost the only wine.

The effect of this on those who kept wine cellars is pretty clear, as champagne and whisky are now almost entirely in proprietary brands, and there is not much advantage in laying them down. A man ordering champagne asks for certain growers and years and takes no particular chances. His wine merchant will keep the wine much better than he can, but with clarets and burgundies it is different, for the choice is enormous, and a man can back his fancy and gain a reputation on his cellar. I am told that people are not giving up their cellars but simply ceasing to maintain their stock. Port is almost the only wine that people still lay down in quantities. Port is drunk a good deal now, not so much after dinner as before lunch. It is much more common than cocktails in the best clubs between twelve and one. But cellars are sure to die out in London houses, one good reason being that people nowadays are continually letting their houses and do not care to leave their wine. Butlers are also become an extinct race.

July 31 1926

PROHIBITION IN THE UNITED STATES

Eight years after the Prohibition Law came into effect the debate on the desirability of the experiment continues with hardly diminished vigour. Day after day the newspapers devote columns to reports of speeches, pamphlets, and books on the subject. Each broadside from one camp is promptly followed by a reply from the other, in which statistical statements are attacked and generalisations are denied.

I have just returned from a 7,000 mile journey through the South and Middle West, in the course of which I made a careful attempt to find out what is happening under Prohibition; and as a result I am strongly impressed by the fact that no single generalisation can possibly cover 'the truth' about Prohibition. There is not one truth, but a score of them. Conditions along any of the four borders of the United States differ from those in the interior. The large cities have one attitude and the smaller towns another. There are notable variations as between the classes in the same community.

The workmen

It seems clear that the average working man is drinking much less than formerly. The great improvement in his material prosperity (real wages have increased about 30 per cent since 1914) is due to several factors, among which Prohibition is perhaps third or fourth in importance. It must be remembered that beer and wine are practically non-existent in the United Stated today. The staple commodities of the bootleggers are gin and whisky, and these are so expensive that the working man, even with extra money in his pocket, simply cannot afford them in large quantities. While there are numbers of 'speakeasies' (illicit saloons) most of these do not encourage the working man's trade, since he has not enough money to interest their proprietors. Boisterous conduct, of the kind once habitual in low-grade saloons, is instantly halted in the 'speakeasy' because it is likely to bring the unwelcome attentions of the police or, in cases where the police have been bribed, those of indignant citizens making public complaints of an awkward character. The vicious system of treating, requiring each man in a group to buy in his turn a round of drinks, has also been discouraged; the average drinking-place does not welcome the entrance of more than two or three patrons at a time. In consequence, fewer men go on a Saturday night debauch and spend all their week's earnings. The percentage of factory employees who miss work on Monday because of drunkenness is enormously decreased.

Middle-class women and men

Members of the middle class in large cities are probably drinking more than before Prohibition came into effect. This is the result of social change which can only partially be laid at the door of the Eighteenth Amendment* since it is seen also in other countries where the sale of liquor is openly permitted. The emancipation of women, which has made such rapid strides in America in recent years, has resulted in their demanding the right to share the recreations of the male, including the consumption of alcoholic beverages. In innumerable homes cocktails before dinner are now a matter of daily routine, though they were hardly ever served in the old days.

As to whether the men in this class drink more or less than before it is almost impossible to obtain reliable data. My own surmise would be that they are more temperate than formerly. One reason for this, almost never referred to, is the universal use of the automobile. Only an exceptionally foolish individual will risk his life by driving in congested traffic when he is befuddled. For many years, moreover, the typical American has been moving away from the habit of indulging to excess either in food or drink. The daily consumption of brandy or rum habitual to our great-grandfathers is hardly known at present, just as no American gorges himself with the vast quantities of food which were once consumed.

As for persons of wealth, the evidence seems to indicate that they drink about as much as they ever did. These are the homes in which visiting British novelists are entertained, and it is on the basis of such visits that they send back their wholly unreliable reports on the Prohibition question. The man of wealth is still able to serve wine either from his pre-Prohibition cellar, or purchased at high prices.

Young people

The much-discussed drinking on the part of young people seems to be an over-advertised phenomenon. It is true that young women now claim their brothers' privilege of occasionally drinking too much and making an unpleasant public exhibition of themselves; but those who behave in this way are a small minority, probably not more than five per cent, and are the modern equivalent for the similar proportion of every generation which misbehaves.

For a few years after the war there was a recklessness in the air which affected young people as well as their elders; and the situation was complicated by the fact that American youth is definitely entering upon an era of altered sexual standards. But hard drinking was never as important as we were led to believe; and it passed its peak not later than the year 1925.

The quality of liquor

The quality of liquor which is being consumed in America today varies inversely with the degree of enforcement of the Prohibition law. The harder it is to obtain, the worse is its character. There is much talk in the newspapers about 'poison liquor', and occasional deaths due to this are recorded; but most of these occur among people so ignorant and incompetent that persons of their sort could – and did – poison themselves similarly with furniture polish or rubbing alcohol long before Prohibition had ever been heard of. In such a city as New York, where there is little real attempt at enforcement, whisky and gin of fair quality can be purchased at prices about twice as high as those which prevailed before 1920. Solicitation by bootleggers is as frequent, and almost as open, as that by life insurance agents. 'Speakeasies' abound in certain districts of the city, and only the flimsiest identification is necessary to establish one's self as a customer. If one does not care for their rather depressing atmosphere, and has mislaid the telephone number of one's bootlegger, innumerable grocery stores and drug stores are to be found which are willing to come to one's rescue. Much of the liquor they offer is 'cut' with water; more of it is not smuggled across the border but is industrial alcohol which has been redistilled to make it potable, and some of it is crude synthetic compounds; but on the whole it seems fairly satisfactory to those who buy it.

From our own correspondent, April 5 1928
* EIGHTEENTH AMENDMENT – *ratified on January 16 1919, the Eighteenth Amendment prohibited the making, transporting, and selling of alcoholic beverages. Prohibition ended in December 1933*

* * *

THE ILL-BRED DRINK
Pros and cons of the cocktail

Although, like many other things that beset us, it was known to exist before the war, it was only with the post-war boom that the cocktail habit became familiar in England, and it has remained with the slump. A cocktail in the old dictionaries is a sporting ill-bred horse or person. 'Cocktail' was first used about liquor in the 18th century as a description of beer with a head of foam. The earliest mention in its present meaning that Dr. Murray traces in England is in Thackeray. Mr. Binnie in *The Newcomes* says to Colonel Newcome, 'Did ye ever try a brandy cocktail, Cornel?' The next is in *Tom Brown's School Days*: 'Here, Bill, drink some cocktail.' The earliest American mention of cocktails is in Washington Irving's *Knickerbocker Papers*, and Captain Marryat mentions them in his *Diary in America*. A great American bar-tender, Professor Jerry Thomas, published a book *The Bon Vivant's Companion, or How to Mix Drinks*, in 1862, and in that work the cocktail only has a very small section, and ice is only used in some varieties. His recipe for a 'Marinez' cocktail is as follows:- 'One dash of bitters, two dashes maraschino, one pony of gin, one wineglass of vermouth, two small lumps of ice.' Gum syrup, curacao, orgeat of syrup,* brandy, and sugar were favourite ingredients. The metal shaker in which the liquors and ice are placed and shaken together arrived much later, and then the distinction between the aperitif of the French and the cocktail of the American became clear.

The essentials of a cocktail

A cocktail proper, according to high authorities, should be made with ice and aerated by shaking. It is now rendered in countless varieties. One eminent bar-tender recently published a book giving 324 recipes. Much ingenuity has been used in inventing names for them. The 'Blue Cavalier', 'Broken Spur', 'Cameron's Kick', 'Gimlet', 'Maiden's Blush', 'Pink Rose', and 'Whoopee' are some of the more exotic. The most popular is the Martini, which was originally made of two-thirds of gin and one-third of vermouth, and the Manhattan, which is made of two-thirds whisky and one-third Italian vermouth. There are many other varieties of these two classics, and the custom has become more and more common of adding orange and lemon juices to all sorts of cocktails. In some houses the cocktail is mainly of fruit juice with dashes of whisky or gin and vermouth, with an olive or cherry or morsel of lemon rind on the top. The cocktail is denounced by doctors and wine connoisseurs on the ground that it mixes wine and spirits together, which is an offence to the stomach, and that absinthe, a most powerful nerve stimulant, is sometimes used, and vermouth, which, though very much weaker, is also a nerve stimulant, is commonly used. If it does its work well the cocktail creates a false appetite, with its consequences. If it does not create or increase the appetite for food it increases the appetite for more cocktails.

The question is now gravely argued by our most serious fashionable gossip-writers whether the sandwich and the cocktail are not going to supersede dinner in the circles of which they write. It is impossible, it seems, to dine and go to the theatre, as dinner gets later and later, while plays must end in time for people who have no motor-car to get home. The dinnerless rich apparently do not care for supper, so somewhere in the morning they have more cocktails and bacon and eggs – in short, breakfast. It is also being discovered that these people have now two hours to spare between the time of leaving their office or their millinery or antique shop or their department in a great store, and so some night clubs are changing their existence and becoming early evening clubs with cabarets and cocktails. French dressmakers and hatmakers and jewellers and decorators are now descending on London and competing with our oldest nobility in selling things at hotels and houses, starting the game with a reception where special whale or beche-de-mer** sandwiches and cocktails are provided. Cocktails are now served at most of the mannequin parades in the best Mayfair shops. They are served before business lunches and dinners on any scale as a matter of course, and few hosts have enough strength of mind to ignore them when giving a private party.

Popular with young women

Cocktails are taken by women, especially young women, in London more commonly than any alcoholic drink since the Regency. They are served in most women's clubs, and it is fairly usual for a woman giving a dinner party there to offer cocktails to her guests. We have not come to the time when a woman who does not take a cocktail is thought a little eccentric although we seem fairly near that time with a woman who doesn't smoke. The hotels in the country most frequented by motor-car people have now to provide the cocktail, the most popular drink with young women, and, as the hotel-keeper charges 1s. 6d. or 2s. for a little glass mainly of vermouth (one of the cheapest liquors in his stock), he welcomes and encourages the custom, even though it means that he has to keep ice, which the British hotel-keeper hates to do. The other side of the matter is that most young women of this class drink nothing with their meals. A good many drink a cocktail because it is the fashion, and it is so small and has a cherry, and so it's not so bad and doesn't matter. To the scenes reported in America, where young people have orgies of cocktail-drinking, there seems to be no parallel here. The cocktail may start the mischief, but it is rarely drunk in England to much excess. The habit, indeed, has hardly spread beyond the South of England and is only favoured by the richer classes.

Changed social customs

Considered as a social custom there is this to be said for the cocktail habit, that it meets a requirement of the times. Male mass drinking (which only existed in the middle classes) is breaking up. The Victorian convention of the ladies going upstairs to the drawing-room after dinner to drink tea while the gentlemen lingered over their port is dead, and with it many usages that made for social segregation of the sexes. The new comradeship of men and women and freedom of manners entail that they should spend more and more of their leisure time together, and, sharing the same sports and studies and smoking together, that they should also find an occasional drink that they could partake together, and in the present habits of the majority of the middle classes in England it had to mean an intoxicant. The cocktail, with its icy feel, its mixture of wine, spirit, and fruit flavours, and its daintiness of colour and size, has a strong appeal to women, especially those who know nothing of wine. Its nicety of preparation and ritual of shaking and serving from the shaker make the cocktail seem a drink apart from all others, and as it can be so easily be carried in motor-cars or pleasure boats it fits in with modern nomadic habits. Its attractiveness and its convenience and a certain innocence that comes from its unlikeness to other drinks and something temporary in it circumstances, of course, add to its temptations to the weaker vessels. It is an insidious drink, and the cocktail habit has been denounced as more like drugging than drinking. The drinker is at the mercy of the mixer, and has to take his word for what is in the concoction, whereas with well-bred drinks he knows exactly what he is drinking: so, besides being a mongrel, the cocktail may have a nasty bite.

The case against the cocktail, that 'ill-bred drink', has been put finally by the greatest wine merchant in London in these terrible words. He was speaking of the end of wine-drinking in America. 'The Americans are a curious people,' he said, 'very strange people. To let you understand, they took gin and brandy and vermouth and whisky and lemon and oranges and cherries and olives and sardines and anchovies and goodness knows what, and they mixed them up with ice – *with ice* – and put them into their stomachs. They were not worthy of God's great gift of wine. And God punished them, and condemned them for the rest of their lives to drink nothing but – *raw spirits.*'

March 11 1929

*ORGEAT OF SYRUP – *a sweetened almond syrup used to flavour cocktails*

**BECHE-DE-MER – *boiled, dried, and smoked flesh of sea cucumbers used to make soups*

* * *

THE RETURN OF THE BRIGHT ONES

London's bright young people have returned to town and are giving their minds to serious affairs. In the spring they had pyjama parties in which everyone had to wear pyjamas, bottle parties to which everyone had to bring a bottle, whether it contained krug or Pol Roget or milk or minerals, and many parties in which everyone had to dress like Cleopatra or Antony or characters out of the Apocrypha. There were also gate-crashing parties which had to get into places where the real gentry were being entertained, and midnight bathing parties on the Thames, and treasure hunts when they had to rush about in fast cars and wear green hats, and in other ways carry on the world's work.

A new form of freak party had to be found for the coming season, and invitations are now out for the first of them. The guests are to come dressed as the person they like best in the world. That does not seem very difficult for our modern egoists, for they only need to come as themselves. But some are not satisfied with that, and there is expected to be some heart-burning among popular young men and women who imagine themselves to be the object of much personal admirations. It is said that a number of bright young ladies are getting themselves up as Lord Brentford and a number of young men are getting themselves up as Mr Epstein's 'Night'.

September 24 1929

* * *

POLICEMAN'S ROLE AS LOVER: ENTRY GAINED TO A CLUB

How a police officer, by acting the part of a lover, gained admission to a drinking club was referred to by Sir Arthur Spurgeon, the chairman, at the Croydon County Licensing Sessions yesterday. Sir Arthur was discussing the difficulty of getting information for dealing with drinking clubs, and contended that clubs should come within the purview of the magistrates, and should be subject to greater police control.

Recently, in that division, he said, a club was suspected of being carried on during prohibited hours. To secure the necessary evidence a police officer had to make love to the woman who held an off-licence in a shop below the club premises. The courtship resulted in the officer being recommended by her for membership of the club, and he found enough drinking going on to cause him to call it an abominable place, with more drinking than in any ordinary public-house of about the same size.

February 7 1930

* * *

THE ANONYMOUS TOOL: DRINKS IN SEALED BOTTLES
Rheims and Epernay have recently been making a considerable fuss about the 250th anniversary of one Dom Perignon, an ecclesiastical connoisseur of wines, who not only put bigger and better bubbles into champagne but also devised the right kind of cork for keeping them there. He thereby became an undeniable benefactor of mankind, for though bubbles in wine are a matter of taste stoppers in bottles are a necessity of existence. But I could often wish that mankind had followed Dom Perignon's example and remained content with corks. Why did they bother to invent that flask with the strangely constricted neck wherein a glass marble, borne urgently against a rubber ring by the pressure of gases that would have filled Dom Perignon with acute dismay, sealed the bottle and retained its contents until the marble was banged downwards? A still more pressing problem is why they invented the type of bottle that is sealed by a stout tin cap which is squeezed on to the top of the bottle by machinery. Nearly all minerals and all 'dry gingers', ciders and larger beers, are now delivered in containers of this type – their special beauty being that, in the absence of the correct tool for removing the tin cap, you might just as well try to suck the contents of the bottle through its glass base, because the tin cap successfully resists assault by anything from a

pickaxe to a pocket-knife. The correct tool – a little sort of wrench affair which resembles no other tool known to man and which is the only commercial product that really does 'defy imitation', since it cannot be improvised by the aid of any other gadgets that are common to camp, car, or kitchen – is therefore an inseparable adjunct to your intended entertainment.

Did I say 'inseparable'? Friends and fellow-sufferers, I dropped a brick. So far from being inseparable the wretched thing is never there when wanted, least of all on picnics; there is always a corkscrew on hand, even if it is only part of someone's pocket-knife, but the tool for removing tin caps is an incessant absentee. The corkscrew is the old soldier, inured to campaigns and ready for them; its successor is the blithe new-comer that has not yet learnt to stand steady on parade. This is a matter of common experience; but have you yet realised two other and very odd things about this later, but increasingly important tool? It has no real name of its own; and in the ordinary way it cannot be bought in a shop.

The fact that this anonymous article will be given away, in dingy metal, by purveyors of mineral waters, but if you go into an ordinary ironmonger's shop (having mislaid all the free samples you have hitherto collected) you have to explain first by word and gesture, that you want 'one of those things for opening lager beer bottles'; and then you have to stand by while the assistant indicates that he could supply you with a garden-roller or a felling-axe, but that he has no 'things for opening lager beer bottles' and does not know what sort of shop would include them among its stock-in-trade.

'Cap-removers'

I went to a very splendid purveyor of cutlery in a very large town and, by word and gesture, again explained my errand.

'I know what you want,' said the assistant, 'and we have them in stainless steel and in silver-plate.'

I prepared to embrace the man, but before I could do so he added, 'At the moment we are just out of stock; but I can show you a full selection next Monday.'

'Do not trouble to make promises you cannot keep,' I replied. 'Long before Monday you will be out of stock again; you will have lost the whole lot. I know; I have lost thousands. But tell me one thing before I go: under what name are these articles listed in your catalogues?'

'They are called "cap-removers",' he replied, briskly, being obviously fluent and well trained.

'Then they are miscalled,' said I, severely, 'for "cap-remover" would be an attachment for teaching small boys to raise their hats at the right moment – and in the case of some small boys a useful attachment it would be. But I want a word that is as unmistakably related to bottles and its own function as is the name of that infinitely more obliging instrument the corkscrew.'

He shook his head sadly, and we parted without further conflict.

But I wish somebody could tell me where the butler goes when he wants to buy one of these anonymous tools for the Quality, and what he says when he gets there. For I should like to purchase several dozen for myself and sprinkle them about the home and car. I should also like to buy several gross and tour round the country during fine week-ends selling them, at great personal profit, to distressed picnic parties.

August 15 1932

* * *

AFTER PROHIBITION

There is a common but mistaken belief that the repeal of the Eighteenth Amendment in December, 1933, turned the United States, almost overnight, from a 'dry' into a 'wet' country. The survey published in the current notes of the Temperance Legislation League shows that this belief is far from the truth. In fact, over a large part of the country the sale of liquor is much more strictly controlled than in this country. There are still three States where the sale of all intoxicating liquor is forbidden – Alabama, Arkansas, and Kansas; Arkansas, however, allows 'home brew' for personal consumption, and also allows grape-growers to make wine for sale to the ungodly across the State borders.

Leader, July 24 1935

* * *

ROAD-HOUSES

The economic slump has made several important differences to the user of the King's highway, quite apart from the obvious one that it has driven a number of the poorer lieges back to the use of their legs. One of the new developments is the sudden rise of the road-house. The road-house has come into being for two reasons. First, the motorist in these days wants some place to which he can take his wife, his sister, or his sweetheart that shall be less expensive than the regular main-road hotels and more genteel than the ordinary 'pub'. Many a modern motorist looked round for a happy medium, and at the precise moment the wayside petrol station began to feel the pinch of under-demand and over-supply. Every hundred yards on the big roads there was a scarlet and green galaxy of pumps, and life was precarious. So the enterprising among the petrol-pumped began to toy with the idea of providing refreshments for man as well as car.

That was the germ of the road-house. And the new idea was not only based on an economic truth; it was based on a psychological truth as well. For a motorist, however much time he has at his disposal, is always in a hurry. If he can save minutes on a journey he will gladly waste 20 to commemorate his saving. It follows, therefore, that he will greatly prefer to fill his car and feed himself and his party at one and the same halt rather than make two bites at a cherry that will cost him at least another four minutes in stopping, parking, bill-paying, tipping, and starting-off again.

The pioneeer
The first of the big garages in the South of England that acted on this double economic and psychological principal was the Ace of Spades, on the Kingston By-Pass. It began with an 'olde-worlde', half-timbered cafe on the roadside, and the idea rapidly became so popular that the Ace had to expand itself. It now advertises 'Breakfast, luncheons, teas, dinners, suppers'. There are also gramophone records, wireless music, a cabaret, and dancing. Other road-houses followed the new craze, and

the earlier ones had to work hard to keep their popularity. The Ace, for instance, built a swimming-pool, and founded a swimming club, which was popular indeed during the glorious summer of 1933. Another development is a club separate from the swimming club. The subscription for the latter is usually nominal and there is a separate charge for each bathe. The club, on the other hand, may have a regular annual subscription of one, two, three, or more guineas, and membership entitles the lucky to dance till perhaps three or four in the mornings and special Saturday evenings.

Then the road-house may be an accredited agent for all the best-known gramophone companies, and at any moment a patron may ask to have a record tried out for his or her benefit. In fact, it is no exaggeration to say that this mechanically produced music is the backbone of the road-house. The licensing laws being so peculiar, and the penalties for their evasion so severe, it is not worthwhile attempting to 'push' the reputation of a road-house by means of alcoholic gaiety. Therefore, musical gaiety is enlisted instead, and the temperance beverages that are procurable inside the walls are reinforced by the dissemination of loud and blaring music outside. In winter, when the swimming baths are closed, a new development is the craze for billiards, which is greatly on the increase, and, of course, the dancing floors are more keenly patronised than ever.

Drawbacks

The architecture of the road-house, as a general rule, is its weakest point. The revival of the half-timber is one of the commonest features, and it is always difficult to harmonise a brand-new old-world barn with a five-year-old or 10-year-old garage that has been having a bit of a struggle to make both ends meet. Often at a road-house the visitor has to pick his way through oil-drums, derelict cars, repair-jobs in full swing, packed caravans, and an all-pervading smell of petrol. Then, these hazards safely negotiated, the dazzled vision meets the Sun Bathing Beach, or the Parquet Terrace, or the Pergola Garden, or the Tudor Veranda on which gay wicker chairs, painted red, blue, yellow, green, purple, are scattered round small wooden tables. The nose is assailed with the scent of petrol, the eyes with a mixture of modern smartness and dingy dilapidation, and the ears with a blaring of American music on loud speakers and the incessant rush of passing motor-cars. The last of these is a great problem for the road-house. For if the house is on the main road it must inevitably be forced to hear the racing traffic. And if it is in a secluded by-way, sheltered and leafy and quiet, how can it skim the cream of the passers-by? But the modern motorist, especially the younger generation, does not mind much about noise, and so the road-houses seldom try to hide themselves in sequestered nooks. The ideal place, indeed, seems to be on the junction of as many main roads as can possibly be made to join at one place.

Farther north, nearer the larger cities and the still deeper financial depresses, the road-houses tend more to the provision of cheap but solid meals than to the fripperies of bathing pools and billiard-tables.

The road-house is a new social phenomenon, and in a short while it will settle down and find its feet. There is unquestionably a gap to be filled between the hotel and the public-house, and it is only a matter of time and experience before the best way of filling that gap is evolved.

November 15 1933

* * *

HOME BREW: OLD LANCASHIRE DRINKS

Lancashire cottagers often kept on musty files various recipes for different beverages, some of which were immediately acceptable and some which had to be got used to. Many of them brewed the genuine article, and a glass of real 'whoam's brewed' ale was not to be lightly turned down when offered. Refusal might be construed as an affront to the brew. Fortunately it was seldom offered except to those who could be guaranteed to quaff the contents of the pot and leave no heeltaps.* When bottled the corks had to be firmly tied down lest the kitchen be flooded.

This precaution was also necessary with any brew of 'smo' drink'. 'Yarb beer' was popular; and many varieties of herbs were gathered and used for the purpose of brewing. Perhaps the chief favourite was dandelion, though nettles were plentifully used and were held to cool the blood in spring. Medicinal herbs were brewed as necessary in a jug, which stood simmering on the hob. I once tackled with misgivings a brew which was guaranteed to clear away lumbago as by magic. One hearty drink convinced me that I had taken the complaint too seriously. It was, at any rate, preferable to the medicine.

Some of the more prosperous put down a cask of home-made wine. Not long ago I tasted with some joy a glass of rhubarb wine which was more than 20 years old and which had rested for that length of time in a well-soaked brandy cask. It had almost the full potency of that spirit and the clarity and sparkle of champagne. All I remember of the recipe is that the rhubarb was pushed through the wringing-machine as the first process. What happened between that and lifting the thimble glass I do not know. Other good wines were made when damsons were cheap. Cheapest of all was cowslip wine. The children loved to be sent with a basket to the early spring blooms. I know one or two cottages where it is still made as it ought to be made. I call there occasionally.

T.T, December 5 1933

A HEELTAP – the liquor left at the bottom of a glass after drinking

* * *

BEER AND POLITICS

Is there any connection between the triumph of the Nazi system and the decline of beer drinking in Germany? – a decline of which, according to a League of Nations economic report, lowers the Germans to fifth place among beer-drinking nations. Possibly Bismarck would have regarded the two developments as related. For, though he drank considerable quantities of beer himself, the Iron Chancellor regarded it with suspicion as a beverage of the masses. At the first dinner he ate after crossing the frontier into France in 1870 he was informed by an aide-de-camp that, though wine was abundant, it had been impossible to procure any beer.

'That's no lack,' declared Bismark. 'The excessive consumption of beer is deplorable. It is responsible for most of the democratic nonsense spouted over tavern tables.'

Miscellany, October 30 1934

* * *

THE SHERRY PARTY: MORE ROOM AND MORE MEN
The cocktail party holds its own and has a train of dresses and furniture which perpetuate it. The sherry party has even a stronger hold, since it suffices more or less for the cocktail addict while preserving a rather milder suggestion. Sherry parties, which were postponed, are beginning again, and it is nothing unusual to be asked to two on the same day. One reason for their survival is the matter of space. Sherry glasses take less space and are much more concise than cups of tea, with all their trimmings of spoons and milk and sugar. Further, if one does not sit down to tea it is almost impossible to eat and drink balancing a cup of tea and saucer and conveying cream cake to one's mouth. The sherry glass, with its tit-bit, is much easier and more comfortable. Also, while you must sit for tea you can be made to stand for sherry, with the result that more than twice the number can be asked at a time.

Sherry parties, indeed, must be packed tightly, otherwise there is not the warmth which leads to mingling. On their feet people will move about where they will not change a chair, and thus introductions are dispensed with. Finally, the sherry party brings more men. It is later than tea and can be well fitted into the gap between tea and dinner. Men can come after six, and the difference is great between the former tea party of one sex and the later sherry party of two.

February 8 1936

The navy's grog

Naval tars of the old school must have turned in their graves when the Admiralty announced that arrangements are being made to supply the fleet with more and better ice-cream, for ices and soft drinks are sounding the death-knell of the daily grog ration. The modern bluejacket, in fact, is showing an increasing tendency to collect 21 shillings a quarter instead of taking his grog allowance, and to spend the money on other things than rum. Although the present mixture of rum and water is fairly innocuous when taken in moderation, it has never been popular with some commanding officers. Admiral Jellicoe was among those who considered that it affected the gunnery abilities of his men.

Originally the allowance was half a pint of rum a day, served out neat. But even that amount was insufficient for the thirsty mariners of last century and there was a general practice of buying and selling the ration among the crews. Frequently the rum would be accumulated for weeks in order to provide an ample store for some particular and glorious occasion. Admiral Vernon – 'Old Grog' – checked the trouble by mixing the rum with water, thus producing the liquid still known as grog. Subsequent reformers reduced the daily amount in various stages, helped by the changed tastes and character of the men themselves.

Miscellany, November 3 1938

CHAPTER FIVE
COMMUNITY SPIRIT

WHERE the government of the day had seen the first world war as an excuse to introduce prohibition, the second world war saw members of the cabinet extolling the benefits of drink to the nation. Admittedly, licensing hours were already restricted, but in May 1940, Lord Woolton, the minister for food, said, 'It is the business of the government not only to maintain the life but the morale of the country. If we are to keep up anything like approaching normal life, beer should continue to be in supply, even though it may be beer of the rather weaker variety than the connoisseurs would like.'

While the government may have wanted to keep up the country's spirits, it also realised that it was generating huge amounts of revenue from the drinks industry. Taxes on beer continued rising throughout the war; the price of a pint doubled, but demand continued unabated.

Pubs became centres of the community and class barriers began to break down. More women or 'pint-pot girls' began to venture into what had previously been a male domain and some were employed in the brewing industry. As for the troops, Churchill said those in the front should be entitled to four pints a week, although getting it to them was problematical. In Burma, mobile breweries were tried out, but with little success, while there were also plans to put breweries into ships. Beer was army issue in North Africa and was supplied in cans painted dull green, and on the day of the Normandy landings in June 1944, Spitfires flew over to France with barrels of beer strapped under their wings.

After the war, some soldiers, at least those who had fought in countries such as Italy, came back with a taste for wine. This became cheaper after duty was reduced in 1949, and in 1947 the first duty-free shop opened at Shannon airport in Ireland, with the idea quickly catching on across Europe. The year 1947 also saw the first British meeting of Alcoholics Anonymous, when five people met in a room at the Dorchester Hotel, London. The group, which had been formed in the United States, had published its basic textbook *Alcoholic Anonymous* in 1939 which included the core philosophy of the Twelve Steps of recovery.

* * *

War news for British troops

It was commonly said in the last war that soldiers in the field were the last people to learn what was happening in the war. It is not likely to be the case this time, for special arrangements have been made to give them a chance of hearing news bulletins by wireless.

When our forces arrived here the troops were forbidden to enter cafes, restaurants, and estaminets* except from noon till two and from six till eight. The evening limit has been extended till 9.30, so that the men can listen to the BBC nine o'clock news on the wireless set which nearly every French cafe possesses.

The troops are forbidden to drink anything in public places except beer and light wine. That is no doubt a wise precaution, for the average soldier of today has not got as practised a head as his predecessor of August 1914. The most popular drink in our Regular Army nowadays is no longer beer but tea, and on such men a glass or two of unfamiliar cognac is apt to have effects not foreseen by the victim. The Provost Marshal's department which is charged with Army discipline is fully aware of the fact that military heads are not so seasoned as they used to be, and has been treating the occasional first offender with fatherly leniency, letting him off with a warning and a helping hand to his billet. There have been very few cases, for the conduct of our men since they arrived in France has been excellent.

EA Montague, Our special correspondent
with the British Forces in France,
Somewhere in France, October 21 1939

*ESTAMINET – *a small cafe*

* * *

No more English beer for BEF

NAAFI (Navy, Army, and Air Force Institutes) has decided not to send any more English beer to France for the use of the BEF (British Expeditionary Force), and its present stocks here are almost exhausted. Negotiations have been going on for months, and may yet succeed, for the brewing in France of beer of an English type at a French price. If they fail, the troops will soon have to fall back on French beer and wine.

The difficulty throughout has been price. French beers of varying quality, some of them good, can be bought at three francs a pint. The result was that NAAFI found it hard to sell its big early shipments of English beer at six francs a half-pint, and has got rid of them only by bringing the price progressively down to its present level of three and a half francs a half-pint, at which it makes a loss. The lowest price at which NAAFI could sell without loss would be a little under four and a half francs a half-pint – nearly three times the price of French beer. Naturally there are not many messes which want it at that price. The factors which do most to keep up the price are freight and the cost of bottles.

The need to conserve the supply of barrels, which cannot be recovered by the brewers when they have been emptied, makes it almost impossible to supply the BEF with draught beer.

> *EA Montague, Our Special Correspondent*
> *with the British Forces in France,*
> *Somewhere in France, May 2 1940*

* * *

Plenty of vermouth

Those who like their vermouth sweet need not fear a shortage on account of Italy's entry into the war. It can be produced anywhere. There is, indeed, a vermouth factory just outside London. The recipe for this aperitif is grape wine to which is added a mixture of aromatic herbs.

Eight years ago the Turin courts had to decide what is a Martini cocktail. It was argued on one side that a cocktail could only be called by that name if made with Martini vermouth. The other side maintained that the cocktail was invented by a barman named Martinez, who named it not merely after himself but after the patron saint of New Orleans, where he worked in 1889. Martini, who said the first Martini cocktail was served in 1877, won the case.

> *June 26 1940*

* * *

Thirsty work

According to the press descriptions which are spoon-fed to the people of Germany, the south-east of the island is either a completely evacuated area or else the inhabitants spend nearly all their time cowering in air-raid shelters. Yet that can hardly be the impression that pilots of the Luftwaffe bear with them when they come over here, for judging by repeated items of information in our own newspapers one frequent assumption of some who have descended in comparative safety is that they can now connect with all speed with what they evidently regard as a well-earned drink. So far from being a devastated area, some of these visitors evidently regard this country as a good pull-up for airmen, a large and hospitable area of licensed premises. What is more, they seem to get their drinks. The first words from one of last weekend's windfalls was 'What about a pint of beer?' whereupon his captors took him to an inn and supplied him with refreshment before handing him over to the police.

How did he know it was opening time, and what would have happened if his arrival had been 'out of hours'? Is our island hospitality such that there is special provision in the licensing regulations for drinks for German airmen under such conditions? Or do they time their descents in order to put in 'a quick one' without running any risk of breaking the law? In any event, some of them seem to be pretty confident that a drink will be forthcoming, and they cannot have got that impression from the pictures that Dr Joe Goebbels paints of this supposedly demoralised isle.

Miscellany, August 19 1940

The Nazis and beer

It is interesting, if not curious, that the weight of Nazi official opinion should suddenly have been thrown against the traditional drink of the German people, beer. The German Ministry of Health has been advocating the use of non-alcoholic beer for years; now it is joined by the Army, the Hitler Youth Movement, and (most surprisingly) by the unascetic Dr Ley, the head of the German Labour Front. It is true that this year there is shortage of the brewers' raw materials, which come largely from Central and South-eastern Europe. But whatever the reason for the access of virtue, the question of an alternative to beer has been quite firmly put to the brewers by the Nazi authorities.

The *Frankfurter Zeitung* devotes a long article to it, concludes that 'a new national drink is necessary', and declares that 'the beverage industry must now prove its worth'. In the year of the Olympic Games, 1936, German chemists produced a popular 'soft drink' called 'Barrel Brew' of 'Olympic Fizz', made from syrup, sugar, apples, carbonated water, and beer colouring. This is held to point the way the *Frankfurter Zeitung* reports that experiments are being made, and speculates whether 'one might use the waste products of cider production or potatoes as a base for non-alcoholic "spirits" instead of for distilled liquor.' Who can say that the German chemists will not succeed and the Central Bureau for National Health of the Nazi party will not yet find something to meet its specification of 'a national drink which fills all the demands of taste, thirst-quenching and refreshment, while at the same time comparing favourably with beer in price, quality, and quantity of production'? Then, given the usual Nazi methods of enforcement, the day of beer would surely be over and the Germans would become soberer and, it is to be hoped, wiser.

August 27 1940

* * *

WHO EATS IN SOHO?

'Open for lunch only.' The sign began to appear some time in September on the doors of most of the foreign restaurants in and around Soho, just as during the previous June another sign appeared on the same doors, 'This restaurant is under British management' or 'The proprietor is a British subject.' In some cases Soho restaurants suddenly 'went Swiss' after having built up their reputation on spaghetti and ravioli and minestrone and bottles of chianti. Soho is not a part of London that has suffered exceptionally heavy damage in the big bombings of last autumn, but a few houses are 'down' here and there.

Dinners served again

Soho was London's escape from English cooking and Soho has bravely carried on with its mission. And after the worst of the 'blitz' was over in November many of the restaurants tentatively opened for dinner, and in many cases it paid them to do so. Officers on leave and a good number of De Gaulle officers and the more cosmopolitan members of the BBC – where the oddest hours are kept – availed themselves of the opportunities offered them by these bolder Soho proprietors.

Despite increasing food difficulties and restrictions, the standard of cooking is still good in the better-class Soho restaurants. A good filet de sole is not a rarity yet, nor a navarin d'agneau; and French chefs have always been noted for their ingenuity in making potatoes interesting. And even if the rarer French vegetables are lacking, potatoes and carrots and sprouts are always plentiful, and cooked in the French way.

A favourite haunt with the lower French ranks, with soldiers and sailors, is the York Minster public-house, off Greek Street, where also a blend of English and Continental cooking is available. Altogether, Continental cooking and drinking are restricted by present-day conditions. Although every Soho proprietor will claim that he has (or can get) enough French or Italian wine to last him at least two years, prices on wine lists have been changed at least twice since the beginning of the war, and since the fall of France there has been an acceleration in the rise in wine-list prices. Therefore more beer is probably drunk in Soho now than in all its history. And the same applies to food; the raw materials available do not always lend themselves to a characteristically Continental treatment. Even served by a Frenchman, a leg of mutton is a leg of mutton for all that.

From our London staff, March 4 1941

* * *

SCOTCH GOES WEST

Some 80 per cent of all the whisky in Scotland, it has just been announced, has been 'dispersed' to regions remote from distilleries so that it may be out of the way of enemy bombers. But even then the Luftwaffe had its lucky shots, for a stray bomb caught a whisky dump away in one of the wildest parts of Caledonia and 70,000 gallons of the precious fluid went up in the resulting explosion. That may be a relatively small amount of the millions of gallons that have been so dispersed, but it sounds a very 'large Scotch' to have been disposed of at a single swoop. And now there is to be no more Scotch whisky manufactured; when the 1942 quota has been accounted for distilling is to cease for the duration of the war.

'Softer' assortments

On the other hand, the making of 'soft' drinks will continue though in 1943 only 21 specified varieties will be allowed. Ginger beer is on the permitted list, and so are grape-fruit and other familiar squashes and cordials; soda water, too, is safe if anyone can raise the whisky (or even the milk) to go with it.

Miscellany, December 18 1942

* * *

THE WOMEN'S SERVICES: SLANDERS REFUSED

Malicious tales of immorality and drunkenness in the Women's Services are 'a vast superstructure of slander raised on a small foundation of fact,' declares the Government Committee which has been investigating conditions in the ATS, WRNS and the WAAF.

The committee, in a long report of great interest, traces the changed standards of sexual behaviour of the present generation, whose 'bravado' talk is described as 'shock tactics' against Victorian 'shibboleths and conventions', and it considers that the vague and sweeping charges made are deeply wounding to the women and bitterly resented by Service men.

Targets for careless talk

'Virtue has no gossip value,' says the committee. The British though they fight so well, are not a military race. They have a deep-rooted prejudice against uniforms. So the woman in uniform becomes an easy target for careless talk. To be seen drinking a glass of beer in a public-house is to provide a text for fluent remarks about the low standards of the Services.

'Shock tactics' against convention

It may be said that pregnancy figures are in themselves inconclusive as to standards of morality. On this the Committee comments:

The use of contraceptives of recent years has spread through all classes of society and sexual intercourse may be common without pregnancy resulting. Standards of sexual behaviour have changed greatly in the last generation and some people today conduct their lives on principles remote from those termed Victorian.

The reticences and inhibitions of the Victorian period have been swept away to be replaced by frank and open discussion of matters formerly regarded as unmentionable.

Similarly with drinking. Though statistics show a steady fall in drunkenness, liquor flows, not necessarily to excess, in a volume unknown in the past. In recent years cocktail parties, bottle parties, road houses, public-houses, and bars cater for the taste of every stratum of society.

Alcohol has become a symbol of conviviality for women no less than men and has set a standard of social intercourse among people of all ages. Repeated rounds of cocktails involve a substantial consumption of spirits and they are drunk by many girls who at heart would prefer a soft drink but fear to be dubbed 'not a sport' if they ask for lemonade or ginger beer.

In 1918 wild and fantastic tales were in circulation about the immorality of the WAACS in France: tales almost identical in substance with those current about the Women's Services during the present war.

September 3 1942

* * *

THE VANISHING GLASS

From the taverns of London comes a story of beer glasses which 'explode' – and with marvellous self-restraint no one has so far publicly proclaimed that Hitler's secret weapon is with us at last. But the glasses do not go off with a bang; their tendency is rather to crumble and disintegrate, apparently under the provocation of some neighbouring change in temperature. The explanation offered is that these are war-time receptacles of toughened glass which can be dropped without breaking, but if they have been toughened too much in manufacture 'a strain is set up' which, suddenly resolving itself, may whisk the container away in fine dust even while the customer is drinking from it. That seems to put a premium on quick drinking –

> *Let the toast pass!*
> *Drink the lass*
> *Before we are lacking both liquor and glass!*

But the explanation of this embarrassing behaviour on the part of the unstable glass, though it may be scientific, falls short in charm. Surely we have here fairy glass that is akin to the fairy gold which thwarts its bewitched possessor by turning into dust and dross; or Puck's own tankard that would baffle the drinker better than any roasted crab lurking in a gossip's bowl. Or glass has been said to shiver into fragments at the sound of some master-note in music; how if some magician has the knack of shattering beer-mugs at the word, or note, of command. If he also happens to be a militant teetotaller his secret weapon may to some people sound as formidable as any that Hitler could evolve.

Leader, February 14 1944

* * *

'MISLEADING' WINE LABELS: NEW MINISTRY ORDER
Sir Ben Smith, the Food Minister, has made an order insisting on clearer labelling of British wines and spirits containing no more than 40 per cent proof spirit. He had received complaints, he said, of exorbitant prices being charged for products that were little more than cider coloured, flavoured, and slightly fortified. He had no objection to such products being sold as long as the public knew what it was getting.

The new labelling order, means that unless a British wine is derived wholly from grapes it will be an offence to label it to imply that it resembles an imported wine or to label it simply 'wine' without a qualifying word describing the fruit used.

Also in the case of British wines and spirituous liquors of not more than 40 per cent proof spirit, the order requires a declaration of the alcohol content, which will help particularly buyers of the cocktail kind of drink. Sir Ben hoped the public would take this announcement as a warning that there were some poor concoctions on sale under misleading labels at exorbitant prices.

December 12 1945

* * *

BOTTLE SHORTAGE

Many thousands of milk bottles vanish every year, and now it appears that beer bottles are in even worse case because, in addition to all those that are mislaid on the home front, there are millions which have been sent to troops overseas, and few of those ever return to this country. So beer-drinkers have been warned that if they do not return their empties they may suffer for it by inability to get bottled beer at Christmas. The warning, issued last week-end, does not give them much time to mend their ways. Whisky bottles, no doubt, are unaffected; most of those are probably in the United States, together with most of the whisky. The habit of throwing bottles into the sea with sealed messages must also account for a certain number of absentees. It is, however, improbable that any sudden influx of that 'bottle post' on our shores will do much to solve the Christmas problem of beer-bottles.

Miscellany, December 17 1945

* * *

CULTURE UNDER A CLOUD

'Poetry in the pub' has been the basis of some promising recitals in the London area and elsewhere, but it should not be combined with drinking after hours. That is the obvious moral of the case from the picturesque Lancashire village of Holcombe, which nestles beneath the hill of the same name; the magistrates imposed heavy fines and refused to be impressed by the explanation that the culprit 'had stayed after the closing hours to listen to one of the company reciting extracts from *Macbeth*'.

It must have been a bitter blow (in more senses than one) to the Shakespearean enthusiasts; but if the *Macbeth* grew so belated the beer should have been omitted. On hearing what it cost them some member of the exasperated company might have been accused for announcing his determination to abandon beer in favour of a fluid outside the Excise regulations; he might have given further proof of his passion for the Immortal Bard by declaring with Hamlet –

> *Now could I drink hot blood,*
> *And do such business as the bitter day*
> *Would quake to look on!*

Better a bitter day than an illegally bitter evening.

Miscellany, October 20 1945

* * *

BOUQUETS FOR MEMBERS

The refreshment department of the House of Commons has taken in hand the delicate task of forming members' taste for wine. 'For the benefit of members who, due to the war years, are out of touch with recent vintages, the following notes are attached,' says the House of Commons' wine list. The wines of Burgundy and Bordeaux in 1937 have, it seems, fulfilled their early promise and are now robust full-bodied wines. The following year was good but not exceptional. Burgundies of 1939 have a low degree.

The Burgundies of 1940 have been destroyed but clarets of the same year have developed greatly in bottle. One need not dwell on the vintages of 1941, though some of the white Bordeaux is said to be very fair, but 1942 was good and 1943 extremely good. Rain upset the harvest of 1944, but 1945 was a wonderful year for quality, though not for quantity. In terms of cash a bottle of 1941 Burgundy costs a member of Parliament 23s. 6d. and a 1943 Burgundy 31s.

June 16 1947

* * *

ACCENT ON 'SCOTCH'

When is Scotch whisky Scotch and who has a right to say so? This, which to Britain is considerably more than a $64,000 question, is being argued to-day in a hearing in Washington of the Alcohol Tax Unit of the Bureau of Internal Revenue.

American distillers are pleading for permission to label as 'Scotch' American whisky made by the same formula as Scotch whisky. At present American law requires them to label such stuff as 'Scotch type'. The 'Scotch type' American whisky industry got under way during the war as an effort to supply the inveterate Scotch drinkers with something faintly reminiscent of Scotland. This effort was regarded at the time as a patriotic undertaking and American distillers saw their chance to establish a local Scotch industry. They were inhibited by the lack of a tradition of 'Scotch type' connoisseurs and tried to foster it by saying that their whisky is as good as Scotch, if not better. By this reasoning they are demanding the right to use the name of what they consider an inferior product.

'Debased in age and content'

Mr. Oscar Coz, an attorney for the distillers, said to-day that the native Scotch drink 'has been debased both as to age and to content without notice to the American consumer.' He complained that foreign distillers are using younger whiskies, some not more than three years old, while leaving the American consumer with the pitiful illusion that he is drinking eight-year-old Scotch. Distillers in Scotland, said Mr. Cox (who did fine service for Britain during the war as a legal protagonist for lend-lease), ought to be compelled to abide by American labelling conditions. When they do not, the American consumer is deceived and confused. The case got off to a fine dogmatic start yesterday with the testimony of Mr. John Nicolson, of Glasgow, who is described as a 'consultant of the Scotch Whisky Association'. Scotch whisky, he pronounced, 'is whisky produced in Scotland'. Speaking with what the papers here call 'a clipped accent,' Mr. Nicholson disdained to make judgments of better or worse, 'though, of course, I may have some ideas of my own'. He devoted his time to elaborating on his first bold thesis with such snappy variation as 'Irish whisky is whisky produced in Ireland and Canadian whisky is whisky produced in Canada.'

This logic evades the American distillers, who insist that Scotch whisky, inferior type, is produced in Scotland,

and Scotch whisky, superior type, is produced in the United States.

Alistair Cooke, January 20 1948

* * *

Doctors, friends of wine

Interest and amusement have been caused by a congress of 'Doctors, friends of wine,' which has taken place at Bordeaux under the chairmanship of the dean of the medical faculty of the university there. This was the second congress of its kind in the city, the first having been in 1933; a further meeting is planned for 1950 in Rheims.

Numerous and varied arguments in support of wine drinking were adduced by the assembled professors. They said that it was the 'best weapon with which to fight alcoholism,' that it contains phosphorus, that 'every French athlete of the front rank drinks it' and that, water being by nature suspect, wine provides the indispensable antiseptic.

Some professors raised their voices in caution on the danger of certain wines to the liver, but the sense of the meeting was definitely against them. The 'doctors, friend of wine' then issued a pronouncement that the following quantities of wine should be consumed daily by the following categories of human beings:

Manual workers (out of doors), one litre and a half; manual workers (indoors), one litre; brain workers and women, three quarters of a litre – these quantities to be drunk during meals. (A table bottle of French wine normally contains three quarters of a litre.)

September 14 1949

CHAPTER SIX

FROM GRAIN TO GRAPE

HAROLD Macmillan fought and won the 1959 general election on the slogan 'You've never had it so good' and for many the 1950s was indeed a time of rising affluence. People of all classes now had a little more money to spend on leisure and consumer goods. Some even began to venture abroad for their holidays, bringing their foreign tastes in food and wine back home.

Articulating these new culinary experiences was the writer Elizabeth David. Her influence was such that 'It is no exaggeration to say that for middle-class British people of the second half of the century, she did more to change their way of life than any poet, novelist or dramatist of our time,' as Richard Boston wrote in an appreciation, on her death in 1992.

Through her books, David urged the aspirational class to 'lift up your eyes to the continent' and some began to adopt bits of the Mediterranean lifestyle including drinking wine with meals. The fact that at the beginning of the decade many of her ingredients such as olive oil and aubergines were hard to obtain, and that food rationing didn't end until 1954, did not dampen enthusiasm for the books. Also appearing in the early 1950s was the first edition of Raymond Postgate's *Good Food Guide*, a reaction to the 'intolerable' food served in many British restaurants, as well as *The Plain Man's Guide to Wine* in which he aimed to provide a jargon-free alternative to books written by 'wine snobs'.

As wine drinking became more popular the *Guardian* began to publish surveys of the grape-growing areas of the world as well as advising its readers as to what to buy. The paper itself though, according to Geoffrey Taylor, author of *Changing Faces: A history of the Guardian 1956-88*, 'traditionally disfavoured the whiff of alcohol', and while sub-editors and reporters would drink, it just wasn't part of the paper's culture. Alastair Hetherington, editor from 1956-1975, was famous for his abstemiousness. On one occasion, when Alistair Cooke, then the *Guardian*'s US correspondent, was visiting England in the late 1950s, Hetherington took him to the Athenaeum club and, pushing the boat out, inquired after a quarter bottle of claret. As for the food, Cooke later said, it 'still immortalises English club food between the wars'.

Following a rise in beer drinking during the war, post-1945 it began to fall. Pubs were closing and the ones that remained developed lounges and beer gardens in a bid to try to attract more than just the traditional male drinker. The general move away from darker, heavier beer to lighter, sparkling ones continued and sales of bottled beer vastly increased. In part this was because bottled beers were usually of better quality than the draught variety but also there was more drinking in the home, no doubt linked to the rise in sales of television sets.

Beyond this, as the *Brewing Trade Review* pointed out in 1954, the public, and in particular young people, had become 'container conscious'; a bottle of something representing unadulterated cleanliness. One of the increasingly popular drinks was lager, which was often served with lime. This had been brewed in the UK since the late 19th century by the likes of Tennent's in Glasgow, but after the war Carlsberg and Tuborg also entered the market. Other British brewers began to brew their own, complete with Scandinavian-sounding names such as Skol.

It was the introduction of Carling Black Label lager though by a Canadian called Edward Plunket Taylor that set in motion a chain of events that would change drinking in Britain forever. In 1953, after doing a deal with Hope & Anchor, a brewery in Sheffield, Taylor was able to distribute the beer through their 200 tied houses. From this bridgehead, Taylor planned to create a national brewery group in Britain and he set about a vigorous programme of acquisitions and mergers, creating United Breweries.

British brewers eventually woke up to the fact that if they were to compete with Taylor they would have to merge. By the end of the 1950s there were essentially six huge breweries controlling both what people drank and where they did it.

* * *

WINE IN THE KITCHEN

Cookery books are of two kinds, the ornamental and the useful, those which make good reading and those which make good books. *French Country Cooking*, by Elizabeth David (Lehmann, 12s 6d) is chiefly of the former kind. It partly consists of quotations from other books, most, but not all of them acknowledged, and most chiefly of literary interest.

Perhaps the chapter in the book which contains the most valuable practical suggestions is the one about the use of wine in the kitchen, though I cannot agree with Mrs David's statement, in another place, that French peasants put wine into the soup when they are making it. I have known them to pour wine into the soup when it is made, but never to use wine in making it. Mrs David is indeed sometimes a little sketchy about wine. For instance, the only Pouilly which has with difficulty obtained the right to call itself a Burgundy is Pouilly Fuisse, and Graves is not a Burgundy but a Bordeaux wine, as Pouilly is a Loire wine.

I cannot think that Mrs David has tried actually to make many of the dishes for which she gives recipes. If she had she would have discovered that four to five pints of water in a soup for four people is excessive, and that to add any water to mussels in their cooking is wrong. Excessive also, and extravagant as well, would be the use of two pounds of French beans, two pounds of green peas, and 12 carrots, as well as turnips and onions, in a 'potee' for six people, or to chop up two bunches of watercress for a potato and watercress soup, or to take as much as a teacup of capers, to prepare Mackerel en Papillotes for four persons. As for beating the yolks of four eggs to put into a soup, or covering red mullet – which, by the way, should never be cleaned out – with melted butter before grilling them, and thus allowing the butter to be lost, or pounding up a whole partridge or pheasant to make a soup – all these are so wasteful as to make my economical French hair stand on end.

The very idea of complicating a choucroute soup by the addition of mushrooms and herbs – which in any case would have no effect in so strongly tasting a dish as choucroute – would make generations of Alsatians and Lorrainers (my father was one) turn in their graves. So would the suggestion that this dish can be ready after simmering for an hour. It requires at least four, and a day is not too long.

Lucie Marion, October 11 1951

'For thy stomach's sake'

Everybody has at least heard of the black stuff that is good for you; an innocent soul can become an invalid temporarily to enjoy port without a twinge; and the teetotaller's conscience is assuaged if his dram is taken for medicinal purposes. The wines of France, white, red, and rosy have so far been drunk only by the unrepentant who like the taste and the effect of the fermented juice and seek no better reason.

But science must rear its respectable head, and so Dr. J.M. Eyland, poet, playwright, doctor, and the first secretary-general of the Medecins Amis des Vins de France, has come to England on a lecture tour to tell the English of the sober qualities of wine. Wine, he says, in tones quite unlike those of the poets of Greece or Rome, not to speak of those of later civilisations – wine should commend itself to doctors, (a) because it is nourishing, (b) because it is a pure product, and (c) because of its therapeutic qualities. He omitted Chesterton's point that it is, like other alcoholic drinks, vegetarian.

The doctor has his first meeting this evening in a Kensington hotel famous for its formidable wine list. No doubt all that he says about the therapeutic qualities of wine is perfectly true (it is an admirable liquid), but one would like to meet a man who orders a bottle because (to quote the explanatory document circulated before the arrival of Dr. Eyland) 'wine given to rabbits will neutralise a lethal dose of sparteine'.

October 30 1951

* * *

COUNTRY DIARY: WESTMORLAND

We reached Lanty Slee's cave by slithering down to the foot of a deserted quarry a thousand feet above the Brathay, swarming up the rough wall to the entrance hold and dropping ten feet into the darkness. This was where this almost legendary figure of long ago made his whisky – the best, they said, for miles around – and apparently not a stone had been touched since we were last here a year ago. Here was where he placed his 'worm', here was the pipe which carried the exhaust steam into the water tank, and the ashes of his last fire – lit perhaps a hundred years ago – are still undisturbed. Here, too, are the ashes of a hundred previous fires and, if you use your torch, you can see the rusted remains of old barrel hoops and underneath the stones at the back of the cave, the airy store for the brimming kegs.

They say the excisemen never discovered this hide-out although they passed scores of times along the ancient smuggler's road which you can see from the cave winding through the fells and down to the sea. Along this road went much of Lanty's whisky, packed in panniers on the backs of ponies led over the passes at dead of night. And the hooves of the ponies as they went trotting through the dark were bound with straw. Sometimes the caravan would meet the ponies dropping into Longdale laden with salmon, great sacks of it, poached from the Duddon, and sometimes, too, there would be scuffles around the Three Shire Stone with the excisemen, a pistol shot, and a body slumped in the heather.

Harry Griffin, October 26 1953

UNFAIR COP FOR NEW YORKERS

Two months ago the New York Police Department stopped hailing weaving motorists and challenging them to exhale, to tiptoe on an imaginary line, and to pronounce in a ringing tone 'the United States Constitution'. The police adopted a device already legally accepted by 50 states, known as the 'drunkometer'.

Under this new system the driver is required to breathe into a small balloon which contains a chemical solution that is purple in its untainted, teetotal state. If the breath has more than 0.1 per cent of alcohol the solution turns to amber. The legality of this device in the state of New York hinges on a percentage; for the state law had pronounced before the invention of the drunkometer that 0.15 per cent of alcohol in the blood seriously impaired a driver's efficiency.

All the motorists who have submitted to this test since it was instituted have had their hearings postponed until the state has made up its mind about the drunkometer's scientific accuracy. Four motorists yesterday doubted it.

Hobson's choice?

The only witness was the inventor, one Dr Rolla Harfer, who heads the Bio-Chemistry Department at the University of Indiana. He could hardly get out his defence of the drunkometer, for the opposing attorneys kept badgering him to the point where he had to confess that he was not a medical doctor and had never made road tests of drivers bearing a suspicious breath.

But the outlook is dim for a return to an old-fashioned 'screening' by an old-fashioned cop. Although the State Supreme Court has ruled that chemical tests for drunken drivers are unconstitutional, a law still stands which says that a suspect driver who refuses to take a chemical test can have his licence taken away. The same thing happens if he pleads guilty.

So an outraged or guiltless man had better volunteer to take the percentage test, which the state says it is unconstitutional to force on him. Any other course is foolhardy, and, besides, there's no percentage in it.

Alistair Cooke, January 21 1954

* * *

DRUNK ON A SENSE OF SIN
To drink or not to drink – that, in Andhra, is the question that may bring down the government. And in Bombay, where prohibition was introduced four years ago, the question has arisen in a different form, with an appeal to the High Court by 11 pharmaceutical concerns against government's proposed control of the sale of 'tinctures and other medical preparations' on teetotalitarian grounds.

The appeal followed a statement in Parliament by the deputy minister of prohibition, which makes interesting reading. According to him, the sales of 'tinctures and other medicinal preparations' in the state had increased more than tenfold since the introduction of prohibition.

The Government, therefore, considered that its duty was to regulate the sale of such 'tinctures' on the grounds that this 'abnormal increase appears to be proof that they are used as beverages rather than drugs'.

During the hearing of the appeal, the Chief Justice of Bombay had to admit in court that 'alcohol has certain medicinal properties' when one of the appellants pointed out that the *British Pharmaceutical Codex* and *Remington's Practice of Pharmacy* – both 'eminent textbooks' – established that alcohol 'stimulates digestion, has a high food value, cools, lifts up, mellows, perfumes, is a sedative and brings down the temperature'.

What government will do in the face of such authorities is in the lap of the courts, but that its attempts to curb drinking – even of tonic and toilet waters – has wide support in India as a whole, is borne out by the new ban in Travancore-Cochin on 'spirituous drugs in "dry" areas'. Travancore-Cochin, it must be remembered, has a socialist minority government which is at the mercy of the slightest impolitic move.

One Swami Sitaran, a social worker, who embarked on a 'fast unto death' in protest against any move to repeal prohibition in the state, was enough to remind the public of the evils of drink; evils which even to many an educated Hindu are deep-rooted. Westernised Hindus who get drunk are prone to do so with vengeance: as one south Indian editor explained once over his n'th drink, 'We drink with a sense of sin.'

April 13 1954

* * *

YOUNG PEOPLE'S DRINKS AT BARS OF DANCE HALLS
Concern was expressed in the House of Commons just before it rose for the summer recess about the marked increase in convictions for drunkenness among young people under 18. For every youth or girl who is arrested, however, there are probably hundreds who think it smart

to spend an evening drinking, and who end up by having had far too much to drink.

For the most part, this drinking does not take place in public houses, where landlords keep a wary eye open for young people under 18 and if they suspect the youth of a customer promptly refuse to serve him – or her. The crowded bars at dance halls, where strict supervision is difficult, tell a different story.

At one such bar in Manchester on a Saturday night, I saw a weird mixture of drinks consumed by young girls and their boy friends. Obviously some of these couples had no idea of how to drink, and changed restlessly from 'long' drinks to 'shorts' and back again, as if feverishly experimenting.

Expensive eating

One girl started with a 'shandy' and a gin-and-orange, went on to a rum (and peppermint?), and then had a stout which she tried to mix with another gin before she had half finished. A youth had a 'black-and-tan' (stout and beer), a whisky, a brown ale, and then, after asking the advice of the barmaid about a cool drink, a bottle of iced lager with a dash of lime-juice. 'The same drink twice is a bit dull,' one girl said. It was an expensive evening for some of them. Admission was 3s 6d each, and with drinks, snacks, and fares, it much have cost some couples about £2 at least.

At first, many of them looked bored even with their drinks in hand, and talked only occasionally, tapping their feet to some private rhythm, but they grew increasingly animated, escaping from their boredom into rival song groups or aggressive exchanges with their neighbours. A few became amorous but usually in the off-hand manner that seemed to be part of the 'Teddy Boys'' code of behaviour.

A couple embraced in the doorway with the wholeheartedness of star-crossed lovers in a Hollywood romance, but they broke off at once when an acquaintance entered, had a chat with him, and then returned to their close embrace. One girl threw her glass on the floor, rose unsteadily to her feet, and then fell over. She got up again with exaggerated dignity and then fell again. A waiter went to her.

Competition for seats

'We didn't have any trouble last week,' said the waiter with an air of pride, but, after he had surveyed the crowded room, he added uneasily: 'It looks as if we're going to get it to-night.' It was competition for seats that finally caused the first incident. When a waiter apparently refused to bring a gin-and-orange for a girl who looked about 15 and was dressed as if she had borrowed heavily from her elder sister's wardrobe, her escort – a youth in the tight-fitting undertaker's black of a 'Teddy Boy' – went to the bar to get one.

Another youth saw the empty seat and tried to carry it away, but was intercepted by the girl, who began to shriek hysterically. Her escort rushed to her rescue and the two youths were soon exchanging ill-directed blows, spurred-on by the group around them. That fight was soon ended when the group was surrounded by burly men in trilby hats whose mere presence seemed to sober. The boys took their seats again with their swagger of savoir faire replaced by youthful embarrassment.

The hall employed at least four 'chuckers out' – as the men in trilbies were called – and in the next hour before the bar closed they were kept fairly busy. Their practice was to wait outside until they were needed, and then to enter with a studied nonchalance and ring the trouble-makers before other patrons could notice. The doorman said they were all ex-policemen and that the management had tried employing ex-wrestlers, but they had treated the 'kids too rough.' 'Of course, I blame the bar for serving the kids,' he added moodily, opening the door for the 'chuckers out' to enter once more.

The bar refused to serve youngsters who obviously had had too much to drink or whom they knew to be under age, but with the 'Teddy Boys" elaborate hair-styles, clothes, and adult mannerisms copied from film stars it was often difficult to make an accurate guess at their age. Girls whose age had been questioned had been known to produce birth certificates – which, in fact, often belonged to older members of the family – to prove they were 18.

Competitive gangs

In the opinion of one of the older 'Teddy Boys' – comparatively elderly at 18 – much of the trouble came from rival gangs of youths who tried to out-drink each other or to impress their girl-friends. 'She's one of the worst trouble-makers,' he said, pointing out a slip of a girl who looked just like an innocent 14-year-old just ready for Sunday school.

That Manchester scene was not unique. I saw it in other large towns where the police had lists of dance-halls, public-houses, and clubs on which they had learned to keep a special watch. It was given an American translation in Warrington, where the United States servicemen are the honey that attract young girls from a radius of at least 20 miles, but the story was much the same. I watched two couples in a public house drink pints of brown ale mixed with red wine which the Americans added from pocket-flasks when the barman was not looking.

The Americans were good-humoured drinkers and made enough noise for 10 'Teddy Boys', but the girls remained bored-looking until Americans began to take an interest in another girl. Then they began to talk and drink nervously, and one of them in a loud voice hotly denied she was only 15. After the girls had had three pints they tottered out on their high heels and the Americans took them to a snack-bar for cups of tea. I saw the girls later vomiting on the train back to Manchester.

First drink at 14

It is difficult to get into conversation with these youngsters – anyone over 21 is shut out by a barrier far more impenetrable that the Iron Curtain – but I was able to learn something about the members of one group in a Blackpool dance-hall after one of the girls had upset a drink over me. The group consisted of two couples all under 18. They were:

A girl, aged 16, who worked in a cotton mill near Manchester. She said she took her first drink at 14, did not like it, but persisted because she found boys considered her 'a drip' if she did not drink. She found now that a drink 'released' her and made her feel 'free'. When she had too much, she stayed the night with a friend because her parents disapproved of her drinking.

A Warrington youth, 17, who worked as a labourer and earned £7-£8 a week. He gave £3 to his mother and spent the rest on clothes, cigarettes, and an evening out with a girl-friend in Warrington or Blackpool. He was rather slightly built and drank stout in the belief that it would increase his weight, but had an occasional whisky to prove he could 'take it'.

A Liverpool girl, who would not give her age but her boy-friend said she was 'about 16'. Her favourite drink was barley wine – 'on two glasses I get a bit giggly' – but she prided herself on drinking the same as her boy-friends. She claimed that made her more popular than girls with more expensive tastes, but she made a point of always drinking spirits when with Americans. Her latest boyfriend wanted to marry her, but she said she had told him 'marriage stinks'.

Youth, 17, who was born in Liverpool and had already had a variety of jobs – clerk, labourer, railway porter, and so on. He boasted about his drinking capacity after several bottles of lager, and when a girl refused to change from gin to lager he told her, 'Be a man,' and roared with laughter. When told he looked American, he preened himself a little and said the Americans got the best girls; the more English you looked 'the less of a break you get.' By about 10pm his mixture of lagers and brown ales had had their effect and he got into a fight with another youth about who should take a girl home. A man separated them without trouble.

August 9 1955

Vodka on the march

There is in America a drink called a Moscow Mule. It is made of vodka, half a lime (juice and all), ice and ginger ale. It will, in future, be increasingly easily procured in this country too, because vodka is now being distilled in the Mile End Road. British vodka will be grain-based, unlike Russian vodka, which is mainly based on potatoes, but it may nevertheless serve as a happy reminder of a certain visit shortly to be concluded:

The distillers attributed the rise of vodka to two causes: its popularity in America, where – perhaps because of the influence of Senator McCarthy – it has, since 1950, made such inroads in the sales of the more conventional drinks that it now ranks third only to whisky and gin: and to the enormous 'Slav' population (by which they presumably mean primarily Poles) in West London. Vodka is sold across the counter now in most West London public-houses. Its greatest virtue is that it can be mixed with almost anything without appreciably affecting the taste (or the aroma) of the base liquid.

April 24 1956

* * *

Barbecue beside a billabong

'We turn the label downwards and no one knows the difference.' As one who serves Australian wine and is proud of the fact, my hostess's words saddened me; prejudice is a long time a-dying.

My first meeting with Australian wine was as inauspicious as could be – in a back street pub in Brighton, where it was reckoned good enough (and cheap enough) for a young man who showed an un-English reluctance to swill beer. My awkward palate did not respond to the port-type Australian red, either. But 20 years later I met Australian wine on its own ground and with a palate educated by French, German, Spanish and Italian mistresses. In those circumstances surrender was absolute.

We had driven out from Adelaide in the blazing sun of the summer's end to a picnic lunch in the Barossa Valley, cooked on a wood fire by the side of a billabong, shaded by a tall, lance-leaved gum tree. The golden light with which the dried-up summer grass fills the South Australian atmosphere came in through the trunks like shafts through a stained glass window, and when I was brought a fino I sceptically attributed some of its purity of colour to this outside influence. I even suspected a taste romanticised by the achievement of a lifetime's ambition to journey through Australia. I need not have done so. It was, indeed, the finest sherry I have ever tasted, and shipped into this country today it costs 21s and tastes just as good.

A chat with the proprietor of the winery (Australians rarely use the term vineyard) made me realise that the barbecue was to be an education in civilised drinking. He was quite properly satisfied with sherry and maintained that a very famous Spanish sherry had been allowed to become too acid in the endeavour to keep abreast of tremendous demand. I agreed. A pity, he thought, because it was such a beautiful wine. Next we would drink claret from the wood, or burgundy (or both), and ultimately Australian brandy.

Mostly, Australians are less appreciative of their wines than they should be. Even at formal dinners it is unusual to find the wines identified on the menu for the benefit of those who have enjoyed them; wine serving in the hotels is perfunctory, and no one bothers about dates. European rituals go too far in the other direction, but they are good publicity. However, Australians are bigger wine drinkers than the British; they drink 1.48 gallons per head per year against our 0.33 (France 21.06, Italy 19.71).

DA Wilson, November 14 1957

* * *

WINES OF THE WORLD

There is no immediate danger that the British will cease to be a beer and tea drinking nation and transfer their loyalty to wine and coffee. For one thing we could hardly stand the distortion of our political economy which would follow such a change. For another, beer and tea (with reasonable amounts of spirits on special occasions) are dictated by history, geography, and climate.

You can ask yourself all sorts of questions on this theme: why are Scotland and Ireland, the United States and Canada the only countries in the world to produce under genuine labels the drink known as whisky or whiskey, both of which come from *uische beatha*, the Gaelic for 'water of life' for which the French is eau de Vie and the Swedish aquavit? Is there not some deep significance in the fact that although the English and the Welsh drink whisky (seldom whiskey) they have never produced anything seriously resembling it, though they have all the ingredients? Does not national character come into it? In spite of everything there are resemblances between the Irish and the Scotch character – a determination to get things done, for one thing; and as an alcoholic drink whiskey most determinedly does things to people.

But leaving out whiskey, the consumption of which declines: beer, also declining, and coffee (increasing gradually, especially under the influence of Espresso bars), what about the British and their wine – in which phrase I by no means include the liquid known as 'British wine'?

Wine-drinking increased by swallows and gulps from year to year. In London, and in some of the larger cities, many of the more respectable public-houses now offer wine as a matter of course, and few hotels of the two star class and above fail to produce a wine list. At this level the choice is small and the labels often deceptive (Oh Beaujolais! Oh Macon! What horrors are committed under your names!) but there it is, a glass of wine across the bar or with your table d'hote often at a surprisingly reasonable price. This was unheard of in many of the same public-houses and hotels even 10 years ago though it did not mean that the Londoner, Mancunian, Novocastrian, or Glaswegian could not find his glass of wine across a counter if he wanted it: all our bigger towns have long been excellently served by wine bars, some of which maintain remarkably good lists and offer surprising bargains.

But the biggest increase in wine drinking has been in restaurants and in the home. They are two very different matters. In the restaurant there is a 'mark-up' of anything from 50 to 200 per cent on wines. This makes it an expensive venture sometimes to buy a modest bottle. Some waiters are as ignorant about wine as some customers, and the use of numbers on the wine list – originally an extension of the use of bin numbers in the cellar – is, in some restaurants, a necessity, for the waiter will merely goggle at you if you go beyond specifying red or white. But there is usually somebody about who knows, and a lot can be learned from researches into even a quite modest list.

A country like this, with no wine laws and no special tradition of wine drinking (except in small, clearly defined classes) offers little help to the new devotee. Where can he look for help when he falls under the spell of the grape? Certainly not, in too many cases, from those who set themselves up as writers about wine. The subject often attracts pretentiousness in about the same way as politics and foreign affairs do.

Take the question of 'wine tastings'. Journalists are invited to many such functions. But many of them are no more than cocktail parties under another label. Whoever heard of genuine wine-tasting at six o'clock in the evening? After a day's eating and smoking and working nobody is in a proper state to taste wine. Tasting is a highly professional matter which depends mainly on the fact that the trained palate has a memory. This palate-memory cannot be developed under stern conditions.

Gerard Fay, November 14 1957

* * *

WHAT PRICE VODKA?

Drunkenness, according to Communist mythology, is a legacy of bourgeois society which will be overcome by proper education of the masses. But the increase in the price of vodka, which has just been decreed by the Soviet Government, shows that alcoholism has not yet been fully replaced by communism. The excessive consumption of alcohol has in fact become a major social problem in the countries of the Soviet block. So much so that it is now a frequent topic in the press and on the radio, as is shown by a survey published in the current issue of East Europe. The article points out that the main cause of concern is the sharp increase in the consumption of hard liquor, coupled with the fact that heavy drinking has spread to the younger age groups and is concentrated in a small proportion of the population in industrial centres. (There are echoes here of what is happening nearer home, dialectical materialism notwithstanding.) In Poland, current consumption of vodka per head is two and a half times higher than it was in 1938. During the first half of 1957 it increased by about 30 per cent. Similar figures of recent increases have been published in Hungary and Czechoslovakia. In all those countries the official press contends that 'uncontrolled drinking' is an important factor in hooliganism, crime, disease and accidents, and a cause of absenteeism and industrial inefficiency. But what is the cause of drinking? The effects of forced industrialisation are probably important – the break up of the family and community life, bad housing, boredom, combined with the Communist assault on traditional values. The old Polish saying, 'Only what I drink is mine,' may ring more true now than ever before. How is it all to be cured? The prohibition of the sale of liquor to young people has already proved ineffective. Increases in price, on the Soviet model, may encourage illicit stills. Vodka is a bad thing, but bad vodka is worse. One Polish writer has recommended Coca-Cola:

'Our "experts" on America resolved to make Coca-Cola a symbol of the great imperialist menace... This is a foolish hatred... The most "imperialistic" Coca-Cola is preferable to the ideologically purest vodka.

If his advice is taken, the wheel of history will have turned full circle. And to see Mr Khrushchev drink his next toast in Coca-Cola would probably cure more than drunkenness.

Leader, January 4 1958

* * *

BUNS AND BEER

The net hanging over the bar at The Widow's Son holds a bag of mouldering buns, over 130 years old, no less, as the regulars in this cosy, brown, sagging Georgian tavern, in the heart of London's East End, are quick to assure the inquiring visitor. And to-morrow, as on every Good Friday for as long as anyone can remember, a sailor will add this year's bun to the net. For his pains – and it is the briefest of ceremonies – the sailor is given £1 and free beer. This rite relies on no records. The East End bun-hanging rests purely on sentiment, on the legend of the widow's son of Bromley-by-Bow. It appears that about 150 years ago a seaman asked his widowed mother to save him a hot cross bun, as he expected to be home on Good Friday. But his ship went down that trip, and the poor lad with it. The mother never lost hope of his rescue, and every Good Friday she added another bun to her pathetic collection. When she died a tavern was built on the site of her cottage in Devons Road, Bromley. The buns were salvaged, however, and hung in a net from the timbered ceiling of the tavern.

Ever since, the publicans, with prosperity, have taken over the old woman's vigil, always asking a seaman home on leave – Royal Navy for choice – to attach the new bun to the remains of its predecessors.

Exposed to the air, the buns soon desiccate, and as they age assume the complexion and texture of a dark dog biscuit. Many of the older buns are in poor condition. The licensee, Mrs. Cecil Hall, whose family have been landlords here for four generations, still quivers with distress at the thought of the night during the blitz when the buns were badly shaken, a few crumbling away to dust, including one baked in the Diamond Jubilee year, as its faded ribbon testified.

The buns were then evacuated for the duration to the disused skittle alley in the cellars. There the bulk of them fused into a rough, black, porous mass. Among those that retained their entity, one noticed that the coronation buns of 1937 and 1953, with medals dangling, and some less august specimens, have weathered remarkably well; somewhat shrivelled, but still unmistakably hot cross buns and carrying their years lightly.

While not in fee to it, Mrs. Hall in the best Easter dole tradition supplements the widow's bun with a custom started by her own family. At midday, after the sailor has popped his bun in the net, Mrs. Hall gives away hot cross buns to regulars and visitors, a hefty distribution, for many tourists come to The Widow's Son on Good Friday morning.

April 3 1958

A NEW HOME-BREWED LAGER

One of the country's leading brewers, Ind Coope, yesterday launched a new brand of lager beer. It is called 'Skol', a short name and a Scandinavian one, virtues when it comes to advertising and to selling lager to people who link lager with Denmark. The flattery extends only to the name; the Ind Coope directors believe that their brew is better than anything the Continent can produce.

In the last few years lager drinking in this country has risen fivefold and though accounting still for only a small percentage of all beer sales, the market shows every sign of growing apace.

The company has invested heavily in modern lager brewing plant at Alloa and Wrexham. A special goblet of Waterford glass has also been introduced to add to the drink's attraction. Ind Coope is even proceeding rapidly to equip its licensed premises with refrigeration plant so that lukewarm lager may no longer be served.

By our Financial Staff, November 14 1957

CHAPTER SEVEN

THE LIGHT STUFF

THE *Guardian* may have declared in 1963 that 'Wine drinking is alcoholic absorption at its most civilised', but the 1960s was to be the decade when bland, gassy beer became the country's drink of choice.

For centuries, beer had been cask-conditioned, that is, it would be delivered to pubs unpasteurised and still 'alive'. This would most likely have been stored in a cellar and then drawn up to the bar by hand pumps; the quality of the beer being dependent on the publican's skill and judgment. During the 1960s though 'brewery-conditioned' beer usually kept in steel kegs became the overwhelming way to deliver beer to the customer. This 'keg beer' was filtered, chilled and a blanket of carbon dioxide added to protect the beer from spoiling as well as providing the sparkle and popular frothy 'head', before being sealed in the container. Rather than a strong arm to deliver the beer to the glass, gas forced the liquid up the pipes so bar staff had merely to press a button on a brightly lit box on the bar.

The first keg beer had actually been delivered to Sheen tennis club, in south-west London, in the 1930s, and Whitbread introduced Tankard in 1955 but by the 1960s beers such as Double Diamond and Courage, sold for more than traditional bitters, were becoming the norm in most pubs.

This white heat of technology was also applied to the delivery of lager. In 1965, Harp, developed by Guinness, became the first draught lager to be available, followed by Carling Black Label. The latter was soon to eclipse the sales of all other beers, particularly among the young. With the British drinking rather more beer than other nations, weaker lager was introduced in the belief that they might not be able to cope with the full-strength continental variety. Whatever the levels of potency, the chances are that the beer would have been produced by one of the big six brewing firms and drunk in one of their pubs (under the tied-house system). In 1967, Edward Plunket Taylor realised his dream by the creation of Bass Charrington, the UK's largest brewer, controlling nearly a fifth of the market.

It wasn't just the beer that was changing but the pub itself. As well as the old hand pumps being ripped out, so too were the Victorian mahogany and engraved windows and mirrors to be replaced by plastic and Formica; there was piped music and the development of themed pubs.

In 1961 the licensing laws were relaxed so that clubs and restaurants throughout the land were granted 'special hours certificates' allowing them to stay open until 2am. It was another political act two years later that was to bring joy to a certain sector of beer drinkers when, in April 1963, Reginald Maudling, the chancellor of the exchequer, abolished archaic restrictions on home brewing. From now on anyone could brew as much beer as they liked, as long as it wasn't for sale.

The most important piece of drinking-related legislation in the 1960s though was the rather more sober Road Traffic Act of 1967. This saw the introduction of the breathalyser and with it a maximum permitted level of alcohol in the blood. Despite having been talked about for a number of years and there being much resistance, an effective media campaign led by Barbara Castle, the minister of transport, saw it accepted. Within the first month, there were claims that there was a 14 per cent drop in serious and fatal road casualties.

In the mid-1960s, Christopher Driver, the *Guardian*'s features editor, began to write a food column under the name Archestratus. With introductions such as 'What London eats today, Manchester eats tomorrow' and 'Lancashire, even its most optimistic moments, has seldom claimed to lead the world in gastronomy', he was perhaps being mischievous and a touch elitist, but it did reflect, along with regular wine writing, a serious approach to food and drink.

* * *

SARDINIAN SHERRY

One of the principal benefits that matrimony confers on the young professional class (which is where my hideout is located) is that it enables us to give up that tiresome pretence of being interested in spiritual and cultural matters – forced on us by our education and our courtship rituals – and lets us settle down to a frank and total absorption in our financial and material circumstances.

When, for instance, you call on the newly married Crumbles – formerly socially-conscious Christopher Crumble and sensitive, musical Lavinia Knudge – do you talk about the problems of secondary education, or English choral music of the 16th century, as you would have done back in the good old days of Crumble and Knudge? You do not. Because Lavinia says…

LAVINIA: Before you do anything else, you must come and look over the flat!

CHRISTOPHER: That's right, just take your coat off – I'll hang it on this automatic coat-rack…

LAVINIA: ... which Christopher made himself, didn't you, darling?

CHRISTOPHER: Got a kit from Rackkitz of Wembley – costs about half the price of an ordinary automatic coat-rack...

LAVINIA: ...and it's fire-resistant too...

CHRISTOPHER: ... now this is the hall, of course...

LAVINIA: ... which we made ourselves by partitioning off part of the bedroom...

CHRISTOPHER: ... with half-inch Doncaster boarding, at a shilling a foot, if you know the right place...

LAVINIA: ... Christopher got it from the brother of an old school-friend of his, didn't you, darling? Now – mind your head on that steel brace – this is the bedroom...

CHRISTOPHER: ...we picked up the bed for a song in a little shop I know in Edmonton...

LAVINIA: ...and fitted it out with a Dormofoam mattress. They're so much the best, of course. In fact there's a waiting list for Dormofoams, but we had tremendous luck and got one ordered for someone who died...

CHRISTOPHER: ... and this is the kitchen opening off the corner here. It was really the handiness of having the kitchen opening directly into the bedroom that made us take the flat...

LAVINIA: ... you should have seen it when we first moved in. But Christopher had the brilliant idea of covering up the holes in the floor with some special asbestos his uncle makes...

CHRISTOPHER: ... so we got a discount on it. We're

frightfully proud of that stainless steel boot-rack, by the way. I don't know whether you saw it recommended in *Which?* Last month…?

LAVINIA: … it's so much more practical than all those silver-plated ones you see in the shops. According to *Which?* they pounded it with 140 average boot-impacts an hour for 17 days before it collapsed…

CHRISTOPHER: … I'd take you out to show you the lavatory, but it is raining rather hard. Remind us you haven't seen it next time you come, won't you, and we'll make a point of it…

LAVINIA: …and here we are in the living-room…

CHRISTOPHER: …have you seen this Plushco plastic carpeting before? We think it's awfully good, don't we, darling? Half the price of ordinary carpet and terrifically hard-wearing. We've had it down, what, two weeks now? Not a sign of wear on it…

LAVINIA: … I see you're looking at all those old books on music and education. You won't believe it, but we had those shelves built for five pounds – timber and all…

CHRISTOPHER: … by a marvellous little man we found by sheerest chance in Muswell Hill. Remind me to give you his address…

LAVINIA: … though I think he did it specially cheaply for us just because he happened to take to us…

CHRISTOPHER: … by the way, would you like a glass of Sardinian sherry?

LAVINIA: … we've developed rather a thing about Sardinian sherry, haven't we, darling?

CHRISTOPHER: … we get it by the gallon from a little shop in Sydenham. Found the place by sheer chance.

LAVINIA: ... tremendously practical, and it works out at six and four a bottle...

CHRISTOPHER: ... incidentally, what do you think we pay for the flat? No, go on, have a guess... Well, I'll tell you – five pounds a week...

LAVINIA: ... it's an absolute bargain, of course. We only found it through a friend of my mother's, who just be sheerest chance happened to be...

CHRISTOPHER: ... I say, you're looking rather groggy. Lavinia, darling, run and fetch him some Asprilux. I don't know whether you've tried Asprilux, but we think it's much better than any of the other brands of aspirin ... No, sit in this chair – it's got a rather ingenious reclining back – we just got the last one to be made. Comfortable, isn't it? What do you think of Lavinia, by the way? Such practical, easy-to-clean hands and feet. You won't believe it, but I picked her up by the sheerest chance at a little bookshop I know down in Wimbledon...

Michael Frayn, February 2 1962

* * *

THE DEMON DRINK IN THE 60S

All other things being equal, liquor always flows from east to west. The other things nearly always are equal. Some Chilean sauternes, it is true, have made their appearance in Manchester, and a whimsical trade in Californian burgundies, sold by the demijohn, flourished on part of the American Atlantic seaboard. But in general, Britain, which is middlemost in this alcoholic drift, imports wine from Europe and exports whisky to the United States. Last year the imports ran to 22 million gallons of wine and the exports to 29 million proof gallons of whisky, which shows that in spite of gracious living and expense accounts we are still a fairly abstemious lot.

This is confirmed by the beer-drinking figures, which have again fallen slightly. Maybe the new style of public-house, with concealed lighting, thick carpets, and drapes on the walls, discomfits a man into ordering sherry or scotch when formerly he would have settled for a pint of bitter. Or more likely, since much of the drinking goes on at home these days, and bottled beer is no substitute for draught, the change simply reflected the emancipation of women and the exhortations of Mr Marples.

Whatever the cause, the phenomenon is welcome. Wine drinking is alcoholic absorption at its most civilised, and it was not the Romans' fault that having given us civil engineering, and at least shown us central heating, they could not make the vine thrive here. Even they had to import from the Continent. Overheads on the cost of imports (including bottling, carriage, and duty) still impose a barrier below which the price of potable wine cannot fail. (Since the duty is 2s 4d equally on a bottle of ordinaire or vintage bottled at the chateau, the customer is getting relatively more than his money's worth for the extra he pays.) It is still possible to buy red wines which taste like a solution of iron filings, and whites which would be better used in lollipops. But the choice of wines is growing and the price of modest enjoyable ones stabilising between 8s and 15s a bottle. Not only Yugoslavia, but Greece, Cyprus, and even Turkey send their vintages westwards towards us. Why should not totally unexpected sources join in, as they would have done if the French had not been there first? Kenya and Tanganyika, for example, could grow vines. How long will it be before we offer our guests a full-bodied red Ngong?

Leader, December 13 1963

* * *

CLERICAL IMBIBERS

A brief tour of the drinking habits of some of the world's greatest clerics is a feature of the latest issue of *The Compleat Imbiber* published today. The Bishop of Southwark, Dr Mervyn Stockwood, writes that he receives more abusive letters when photographs of him drinking are seen in the newspapers than for any other misdemeanour. But he is unrepentant and records that, according to the Pope's Chaplain, 'His Holiness has his siesta in the afternoon and then at five o'clock he has a bottle of champagne.' Geoffrey Fisher, the last Archbishop of Canterbury, Dr Stockwood tells us, made do with rice pudding and prunes washed down with water. The present Archbishop, however, 'mellowed at a Cambridge high table' does justice to a good wine.

Dr Stockwood records that the Patriarch of Russia, who received him and talked for a long time, offered no refreshments, whereas the Ecumenical Patriarch of Constantinople offered a long menu 'and the wines were admirable'. He adds: 'I have drunk sweet coffee and sweet liquers with the Armenian, Coptic and Abyssinian Patriarchs, and I hope that good God has counted it to me for righteousness.' Dr Stockwood's contribution to *The Compleat Imbiber* is called 'Gaiters and Gastronomy', and concludes with some cold words on the fare at confirmations, institutions, and civic functions.

October 5 1964

* * *

CHALLENGE TO MILD AND BITTER
Working men in the North are turning more and more to wine drinking to satisfy their thirsts, judging from the Northern Club Trade Fair which opened at the Winter Gardens, Blackpool, yesterday.

Mr Hugh Graham, editor of the *Club Secretary* which is sponsoring the fair, said he was 'staggered' at the number of inquiries about wine made by secretaries of working men's clubs. Working men, he thought, were just beginning to realise they could afford wines. Many preferred to spend 2s on a glass of wine instead of on beer, although there was some hesitation about buying it by the bottle.

One secretary from a Flintshire club said many of his 900 members had asked for wine after Continental holidays.

The common theme of the 72 stands was a drift towards automated leisure. Everywhere there seemed to be stands renting or selling 'fruit' machines and 'one-armed bandits' (one alone can yield an annual profit of £1,000 to a sizeable club).

October 21 1964

* * *

MARMALADE TEA
Somewhere between Whim and Windy Gowl the radiator suddenly boiled over. There was a wet explosion, a gusher

of brown water and white vapour – not at all the kind of thing one expects from a car in 1964, even in Scotland.

Obviously, I needed a telephone to tell the AA that I was in difficulties again. And the obvious place to find one, and to wait until the arrival of a father-figure in a Land-Rover, was the cottage I could see only about 25 yards farther up the road where several cars were parked beside a sign that said: HIGH TEA.

The Cottage was large and square and grey. There was no relief from all the rectilinearity and sombreness except for the polished brass of a Victorian knocker. I went inside quite unprepared for the scene of gay debauchery that greeted me.

At a table close to a window overlooking roses, four elderly ladies in severe suits and grand matriarchal hats were slowly swaying to and fro, waving slices of muffin, in time with the incomprehensible song that they were singing. There was a suggestion of Gaelic folksiness about the sad melody; the words were long drawn out and slurred at the edges. All four singers seemed to be animated by a compelling sense of rhythm, but evidently no two of them felt it quite the same. One of the four, tilting her chair back on two legs, almost went all the way, convulsively fell forward over her plate to save herself, and caused her hat to fall across her eyes.

'Whee!' she exclaimed. 'That was a near one!' The others stopped singing, more or less, to cheer and to thump the table till the dainty china rattled, and there was a confusion of excited high-pitched giggles.

'Oh my!' protested another, whose pinch-nose spectacles, dangling from a ribbon of watered black silk, were swinging back and forth against her lace bodice. 'Stop for a minute, do, or I fear I may burst!' Tears of merriment were dripping from her long, white, powdery nose.

As the gales of laughter now somewhat abated, one of them called shrilly for the waitress, and one said, 'Yes! Another pot!' and a third simply squealed as if stabbed with an exquisite hatpin of awareness of pleasure.

'Pot,' of course, is an informal expression for marijuana, a narcotic I believed to be illegal in Pentland villages. I dismissed the fantastic suspicion as soon as it was formulated. When the waitress was free again I had to ask her a question.

'What's got into them?' I asked. The waitress, a pleasant-looking woman of middle age, flushed a bit but good-naturedly laughed.

'Oh, them,' she said. 'It's nothing really. It's just the marmalade. They haven't the head for it, the dears.'

'Marmalade? Marmalade for tea?'

'It's no' the regular marmalade, sir,' she said. 'It's the new marmalade.' She laughed again, and her laugh was perhaps a few decibels louder than one usually hears from a waitress on duty. It was a laugh that had quite a bit of guffaw to it. 'The new Scotch whisky marmalade,' she said. 'There's a great call for it these days.' She laughed again. 'Who's want jam?'

A few mornings later I was hardly surprised to read an article in a perfectly sober newspaper substantiating the waitress's explanation. 'New this year,' the *Scotsman* reported, 'is the whisky marmalade from Scotts of Carluke.' Mackie's of Prince's Street said the novelty was proving popular and tourists in particular were 'lapping it up'.

'We've been working on developing whisky marmalade for some time, with the export market in mind,' said Mr Kenneth Scott, speaking over the telephone from his factory in Lanarkshire, 'and now we're selling it in nearly 30 countries. The marmalade is made of Seville oranges. The whisky in it is real Scotch whisky, but of course the alcohol evaporates during the cooking.'

I'm not so sure about that evaporation.

Patrick Skene Catling, December 23 1964

* * *

LAS VEGAS, YORKSHIRE STYLE

It's a long, wet way from Las Vegas; but the Greasbrough social club, standing among sodden fields outside Rotherham, is indubitably something of a boisterous brother-under-the-skin to the more sophisticated Sands Hotel of Nevada.

This week the club, with a membership of 2,000, earned national publicity because of an attempt to get Sammy Davis Jr to appear there. Regulars want to know what all the fuss is about. 'We've had the best before,' says one, 'and we expect only the best. Working men's clubs have changed.'

There's no doubt about it, working men's clubs have changed. 'Who would ever have thought,' says the occupant of a bar in one of Greasbrough's five public houses as he stared out of a window offering a dim and daunting view of the road to smoky Rotherham, 'that a place like this could ever get them?' 'Them' means, in Greasbrough, such as Johnny Ray and Bob Monkhouse. This week Matt Monro is appearing nightly. Adam Faith is to come. Can Sammy Davis Jr really be far behind?

The club is only four years old. It began as a wooden hut but now it has become one of the northern clubland's Taj Mahals. Besides the vast concert room that seats 800 there is a dance hall and a giant lounge. 'It's overwhelming at night,' says a barmaid. 'We've got 24 beer pumps and they're going all the time.' The nightly consumption is formidable and so is the breakage. About 500 new glasses a week are required. The total staff of the club – some responsible for picking up the broken glass – is 50.

The club does not look like a showplace for some of the highest priced entertainers of our time. But it is rumoured that if Sammy Davis Jr does arrive to delight the wives of miners or steelworkers, he will get £2,000 a week; and townsfolk who consider themselves on the inside of things say that Johnny Ray got £1,000 for his week's work.

January 15 1965

* * *

CHANGES IN A CITY'S DRINKING

Bradford has had its drinking habits examined scientifically; and the conclusion issued today is that the city is following the national trend in learning to appreciate the delights of Beaujolais as well as bitter.

The research, which showed wine and spirit drinking to be on the increase in Bradford, was an exercise carried out by students of the management centre of the city's Institute of Technology. They were given a hypothetical problem – that of a European wines and spirits exporter wanting to test market his products in Bradford before selling them nationally.

The researchers 'sampled' nine carefully chosen wards of the city – from Tong to Manningham and from Eccleshill to East Bowling – asking 50 retail traders and 140 adults about their drinking habits. They asked people where they drank, with whom they drank and what they drank. There was also an 'identification' test about the names of red and white wines.

Beer – draught, bottled, and keg – is still Bradford's most popular drink, and only a handful of people said that the last drink they had before the interview was wine. The research also showed that slightly more people drank at home than in public houses – a fact that should appeal to wine merchants interested in persuading people to have wine on their own tables as well as when they dine out.

Bradford, said the researchers, seems likely to follow the trends expected to develop nationally: a 38 per cent rise in the consumption of wines and spirits by 1970 and only 11 per cent increase in beer-drinking. Wines, it points out, are the only market which shows 'growth potential' at present, although vodka sales are promising, possibly because of the city's Polish community.

Bradford showed a preference for white wine over red; no one seemed to think much of rosé. The conclusion of the researchers are that any firm wanting to test-market a wine in the city should choose sweet and white – and preferably below 10s a bottle. And allowance should be made, it suggests, for a 'relatively unsophisticated palate for wine' compared with some areas of the country.

Geoffrey Whiteley, June 1 1966

* * *

B-TEST POSITIVE – BUT ONLY AFTER SPENDING £5 12S 6D

All Fleet Street seems to be staggering around blind drunk these days in order to do its stern journalistic duty. The *Guardian* appears to be the only newspaper which has not sent out half its staff to get conscientiously sozzled over cocktails, wine and brandies at West End restaurants, in order to test the breathalyser in action. A newspaper can lose caste by these omissions.

Accordingly, I suggested to the news editor that it was time we sent someone out to get well fed and half-cut at the firm's expense – and that the someone should be me. 'If you get quarrelsome when you've had a few, write it up at home,' he said dubiously. 'Are you going to write the piece drunk or sober?' asked the assistant news editor, who has to look at things from the practical angle. 'Do it both ways and see which way comes out best,' said a colleague sweetly. Obviously he wished he'd thought of it first.

Refused to stint

I wrote a few preliminary notes so that I would know later in the day what it was I was supposed to be doing. My car was left safely where I would not have to drive it. I bought half a dozen breathalysers (30s) from Gamage's. 'Do you think you can do this on beer?' asked the deputy news editor, always with the practical aspect in mind.

But I refused to stint my stern duty. I took a taxi (2s) to the nearest pub across the street and had the most expensive dry sherry they had (2s 9d). Then, just in case their sherry was not absolutely typical (you have to be exact in this sort of research) I took another taxi (4s) to another pub and had another dry sherry.

Then I unpacked one of my breathalyser kits. Really, you can throw away the actual contents of these packets – if you can understand the instructions you are thoroughly sober. You have to (I quote) 'gently cut off both ends of the glass vial, using the metal glass file supplied, insert the vial into the neck of the plastic bag, with the section of the vial containing the crystals nearest to the plastic bag. The arrow head should be pointing towards the bag. Fit mouthpiece on to the other end of vial.' I followed the instructions and used my breathalyser on my two sherries. It appeared I was unfit to drive already.

But wait! With these do-it-yourself breathalysers you have to wait 15 minutes after taking alcohol or wash your mouth out. Facilities for washing my mouth out being at a premium, I opted for the pause, and found I was still fit to drive.

Encouraged, I took a taxi to the best restaurant I could think of, handsomely tipping the driver (5s 6d). It so happened that a bar was next door to the restaurant, so I nipped in and had a dry sherry (2s 9d). I then got my glass file out again and gave myself another test. At this junction I noticed that people were beginning to look at me curiously. The test, however, indicated that I was only just up to the limit, if that.

I went into the restaurant. So as to produce an absolutely objective and typical result, I had food that was not stodgy nor light – just pricey (sole Louis XIV with creamed potatoes – 16s). Did I forget to mention that I took an old friend with me? She (scallops with cheese sauce 14s) was over the limit on one sherry (2s 9d) and half a bottle of wine (9s 6d). However, after half a bottle of wine on top of my three sherries, I was still only just on the limit.

Most impolite

Strange, because outside in the street people kept bumping into me in a most impolite way. It was past 3pm. Eager to see just what would drive me unequivocally over the limit (one must be prepared to suffer in a good cause) I went pushing on the doors of a few pubs around Covent Garden, which notoriously tend to stay open at all sorts of strange hours. But their doors remained stubbornly closed, so I failed in my ultimate duty.

But perhaps not quite. Half an hour later, without having consumed another drop of alcohol, I gave myself another breathalyser test and found I was now tangibly over the limit. Conclusion at the end of a dutiful (approximately £5 12s 6d) day: it is all a bit of a lottery, and Mrs Castle is right when she says don't drink and drive. However, if you can rely on taxis, it is very nice doing the necessary research.

Tomorrow, I hope to start the first of a series of 367 articles on why newspaper economics are in a mess. With research.

Dennis Barker, January 5 1968

* * *

WINE AS WELL AS FOOD

Two types of men are hard to endure … the ones who insist on looking up your trains for you, and the ones who assume that because you are female you prefer a sweet white wine. Most women who drink wine have views on it, but they still have a diffidence about choosing it ... which is how the women's wine club run by Jean Robertson, Katharine Whitehorn, and Elizabeth Ray (wife of Cyril Ray, the wine and food writer) came into being.

Mrs Robertson, who was half of the *Spectator*'s 'Leslie Adrian', and now writes a similar column of consumer guidance with her husband under their own names for the *New Statesman*, says: 'We feel it logical that the person who chooses the foods and cooks the meal should also be able to choose the wines to go with it, instead of asking her husband to trot off to the pub or the off-licence at the last minute.'

So far the club has about 700 members, mainly middle class, mainly over 30, who pay 10s a year and get wines with trustworthy labels at from 1s to 2s a bottle cheaper. But they too like the social aspect of the club – a Christmas wine and cheese party in London this Thursday was oversubscribed by last week. There are opportunities to go on trips abroad and to wine tastings, which provincial members especially enjoy. Mrs Robertson herself thinks that the education in how to buy and treat wine is the club's most useful function. Item of useful information from her: that sherry keeps more or less indefinitely is a fallacy. Once opened, it should be used up as soon as possible.

Mary Stott, December 12 1967

* * *

COMING TO TERMS WITH THE BREATHALYSER

Five quotes: 'As far as the breath test is concerned, the accident figures don't prove a thing'– Mr Norman De Johns, National President of the Licensed Victuallers' Association.

'It is not my experience that people who have had too much to drink drive fast and dangerously. That is only the experience of members of Parliament apparently. They never consult in matters of this sort with people who have to deal with cases'– Mr Seymour Collins, Metropolitan Police Magistrate, West London Court, December 21.

There has been an upsurge in immorality among teenagers at Christmas, Dr Maurice Packer, secretary of the Bournemouth branch of the Christian Medical Fellowship, has stated in a letter to local newspapers. He pointed out that rather than risk a breathalyser test while driving home from parties at bachelor girls' flats, young men would stay all night. 'Under such circumstances… heightened sexual urges plus diminished discretion plus opportunity…this Christmas could result in blighted lives and lifelong regret. It truly means a period of restraint' – The *Guardian*, December 22.

A London Co-operative Society milkman claimed last night that Essex Police had made him take a breathalyser test at 7.30am on Christmas Day because they heard him singing while he was on his round. The milkman, Mr Samuel Ashworth, aged 60, of Tyrell Drive, Southend, said the test had been completely negative and he had reported the matter to his depot manager. Essex Police said they could not comment on the incident – The *Guardian*, December 28.

'Too much emphasis should not be placed on the new drink law. There may be a number of factors contributing to the drop but there can be little doubt that the law kept many people off the roads' – The RAC commenting on the 60 fewer deaths this Christmas.

Adam Raphael, January 8 1968

* * *

A TOUGHER BREATHALYSER TEST

There is no more litigious defendant than the aggrieved motorist. So it is hardly surprising that the 'breathalyser' law has been attacked frequently in the courts in its two years of life. Passing a new law in an area of social behaviour where habits are deeply ingrained and widespread is like sending in a lame cat to chase some very spry pigeons. Since magistrates and judges are as prone as anyone to break this law (and have indeed been convicted under it), it is easy too to see that many of them should identify readily with the motorist's problem and scrutinise the law with more suspicion than, for example, the Dangerous Drugs Act. It is said also that some magistrates do not like losing their discretionary powers and having to disqualify convicted drivers willy-nilly.

If this explains why the pigeons are spry, something must still be done to make the cat less lame. The idea of the breathalyser law is a good one. As the Minister of Transport, Mr Fred Mulley, has said, the law is operating effectively in general. Ninety-seven per cent of prosecutions result in convictions. In the first few moths after the Act was passed, there was a sharp drop in the number of road accidents. If the early optimism which this aroused has not been fully borne out, as accident statistics have gone up again, this shows only that the Act needs strengthening. To judge from the *Guardian*'s survey of motorists, the only one that a national newspaper has conducted, almost 60 per cent think the Act is too weak.

The weak points seem to be the definition of a driver (a man who parks and goes into a shop is not driving; a man who stopped and went to a lavatory and was stopped by the police on his way back to the car was driving) and the 20-minute rule. Under this latter rule the police cannot test a driver within 20 minutes of his last drink, because 'mouth alcohol' would affect the breathalyser. But since the breathalyser test is only a clue, and the test on which prosecution stands or falls is the subsequent blood or urine test in the police station, this is irrelevant. Mr Mulley has said that a review of road safety is now in progress, and that this could lead to changes in the breathalyser law. But if the law's effectiveness is to be maintained, this could be too slow a timetable. There is already a case for strengthening it. Why delay?

Leader, October 22 1969

CHAPTER EIGHT
THE MORE, THE MERRIER

AMIDST the news of the oil crisis and three-day week, not to mention the growing women's movement, the pages of the *Guardian* in the 1970s carried two columns that eloquently charted the changes going on in the world of drink.

John Arlott was the *Guardian*'s cricket writer but in 1969 began producing a wine column, so the story went, to give him something to do in the winter months when there was no cricket. This was no hack job, though. Arlott was a discerning and enthusiastic wine correspondent, as shown by the fact that when, late in his life, he auctioned much of the contents of his cellar for £29,315. The man himself described this as 'Only the big money stuff I'd choke if I drank …'

As well as recommending what to buy, the columns covered everything from the quality of wine in pubs to changing tastes in drink.

Despite being one of the paper's most distinguished writers, Arlott was always fearful that he might be sacked, particularly with a change in editor. So when Richard Gott was appointed features editor in 1978, Arlott believed the £30 per column he was paid, would soon be coming to an end. Thus he invited Gott out to lunch at the Tate Gallery restaurant. With waitresses frequently bringing out fresh bottles to try, 'John was determined that his new editor should be left in no doubt about his continued suitability for the task of writing about wine', Gott later wrote. He eventually staggered back to the paper's Farringdon Road office and a new contract was soon in the post.

Meanwhile a freelance journalist called Richard Boston who had occasionally written for the paper was commissioned in 1972 by an airline to write a guide to London pubs. As well as discovering that the traditional pub was disappearing, Boston was disgusted by the appalling state of keg beers such as Watney's Red Barrel – perhaps the most reviled of them all. The guide did not appear but when a reader wrote in July 1973 to the *Guardian* enquiring as to why the paper didn't have a column devoted to beer as it did to wine, Boston spotted an opportunity. He pitched the idea (in a pub) of a short series that would have a go at the brewers as well as looking at things such as pub games and architecture, to Mike McNay, the deputy features editor. The answer was 'Good idea. Your round', and 'Boston on beer' began to appear every Saturday.

It was the right time for such a column and letters poured in full of information and suggestions. One week Boston mentioned the Campaign for Real Ale (Camra) and this caused such a surge in their membership that they had to take on extra staff.

A myth grew up that Boston's column led to the setting up of Camra but he claimed hadn't even heard of the group when he started writing about beer. The pressure group had been founded in 1971 by four Mancunians to campaign against, as one of them put it, a few super breweries 'owning all the country's 60,000 pubs and each churning out a similar insipid bastardised beer'. They were skilled at getting their message across; they coined the term 'real ale' to describe cask-conditioned beer and, by staging mock funerals and gathering petitions, the breweries eventually began to take notice and cask-conditioned ale started to re-appear. This has been described as one of the most successful consumer revolts of all time. Possibly too successful for Boston, who found himself typecast; he eventually had to seek solace in a Watney's pub where he knew he wouldn't be bothered by bearded beer bores.

Camra may indeed have started a revolution but the 1970s was the decade when draught lager really began to dominate. This lager may have been a weaker version of its continental cousins but advertising campaigns such as Heineken's ('reaches the parts that other beers cannot reach') combined with the two of the hottest summers on record saw lager sales dramatically rise. Other lagers came along with their own 'witty' adverts, and by the end of the decade lager accounted for 34 per cent of beer sales.

Wine sales were also increasing with branded names such as Blue Nun and Mateus Rosé (with the bottle often ending up as a lamp base) proving particularly popular. Beyond this, most drinks cabinets had a bottle of Martini, the heavily promoted Italian vermouth, and there was a growth in the popularity of neutral-flavoured spirit-based drinks that tasted of something else such as Bailey's Irish Cream.

* * *

Country diary: Lincolnshire

Lincolnshire: A dozen miles south of Lincoln, and at the foot of the west-facing limestone scarp that runs the length of the county, lies Stragglethorpe. The inelegance of the name is redeemed by a pleasant medieval church and a one-and-a-half-acre vineyard, which is, I believe, the most northerly producing vineyard in Europe. Started as a hobby, it is now building up to an annual vintage of about 2,000 bottles. The vines are Seyve-Villard, must frequently used for champagne, but the wine produced here is of a white burgundy type and is labelled as Lincoln Imperial. This yard must be very close to the northern climatic limit for the cultivation of the vine but it proves, as do the other commercial yards in the warmer climate of Hampshire, that viniculture is sadly under-exploited in England today. Until the dissolution of the monasteries in the 16th century and the consequent dispersal of the technical expertise that managed them, southern England had many vineyards. The product was, no doubt, a rough and unsophisticated potion but it is tempting to muse on the different national characteristics which we might have shown had we continued to live as a wine-drinking as opposed to a brewing nation. The gin palace era might not have been avoided but would we, under the complaisant influence of wine, have devised such peculiar national licensing customs? In a country of potatoes grown for packeted crisps, sugar beet to sweeten tea and barley by the acre for malting, the production of wine is a pleasant eccentricity with a scent of what might have been mingling in its delicate bouquet.

Colin Luckhurst, November 21 1970

* * *

ALGERIAN WHISKY

The Algerians are about to start making whisky – which is odd in a teetotal Moslem country which is at the same time digging up its French planted vineyards. There is already Algerian Cognac produced by a Russian-supplied distillery and now the Ministry of Industry has advertised for tenders to supply a distiller capable of producing 'Scotch-type' whisky.

One hopes it is nicer than Danish whisky. The Danes reckon the secret is to throw a handful of peat into some neat alcohol. The result is strangely reminiscent of cheap prohibition hooch.

December 6 1971

* * *

WINE IN A BOX

In an age of packaging, space-consciousness, fork trucks, display and disposability, the wine-box or packet-wine was inevitable. It is called Ronzas Rouge and it is contained in a 'Hypa' Pack.

It claims no more than to be 'genuine French red wine' and if it is not distinguished – and it is not – it is honestly drinkable – round, full, amiable, and completely ordinary. From the vineyards of the Cie Salins du Midi, it is presumably a blend of wines from the Languedoc which produces more wine – often, so far as the French Government is concerned, embarrassingly more – than any other part of France. It makes the vast bulk of their vin ordinaire; and many of the native workmen drink their four or five litres of it a day.

Wine in this area is produced at minimal production cost by extensive mechanisation. The Ronzas is packaged in a modernised plant at Sete, a town better known for the manufacture of vermouth. The burnable box made from a laminate of polythene and cardboard with aluminium ends, measures 3in x 3in x 8in, and holds a litre of wine.

It is opened by piercing a couple of holes in the end and it packs so tidily that you can take it almost anywhere. Because it is 'flash pasteurised' it will never improve for keeping, but it is said to have a long 'shelf life' and retains its flavour for three or four days after it is opened.

It is imported by Bushell Brothers (Wines) of Botolph Lane, London EC3, is being tried by Keymarkets and Tesco Trademarkets; and Old Chelsea Wine Stores have it at 95p the box.

John Arlott, February 22 1973

* * *

LETTER TO THE EDITOR OF WINE AND FOOD
Sir, – Can you please advise me of a non-alcoholic wine suitable for a wedding luncheon? Your help will be most appreciated.

Yours truly,
AL Rogers

March 8 1973

The editor cannot oblige Mr Rogers.

* * *

BRITISH BEER: THE GRIPES OF FROTH
Sir, – It has always been a matter of wonder to me that while the novice in wine-drinking can undergo his novitiate guided by the discriminating palate of John Arlott through your columns, the tyro beer drinker is left to sup his pints with no more guidance than the advertisers' blurbs. It seems to me that it is this refusal to take beer as seriously as wine that has allowed the development of a brewing industry which cares little with a few notable

exceptions for quality and even less for variety. Perhaps the occasional newspaper column by a discriminating beer drinker might help to bring the brewers to their senses?

Stephen Edwards

Twickenham, Middlesex.

July 14 1973

* * *

HERE FOR THE BEER

In 1970 we drank 1.14 gallons of wine per head of adult population, and 29.7 gallons of beer. I imagine that this proportion would be reversed if one was to measure the newspaper column inches devoted to the respective beverages. There are good reasons for this. Precisely because we are not a wine-producing country, fermented grape juice will always be to us something foreign and exotic, and we readily accept the need for expert guidance to it. Personally, though I have a memory that is perfectly adequate for normal purposes, and that retains to this day such useless information as Latin gender rhymes, yet I suffer from amnesia on the subject of whether claret is Burgundy or Bordeaux, and need to be reminded at least once a fortnight – secretly taking comfort in the fact that the French themselves are equally mystified, having no more heard of claret than the Germans have heard of hock.

With beer, on the other hand, it's quite different since everyone who frequents a pub and averages a pint or so a day considers himself the country's leading authority on the decline of British beer, pubs and the moral fibre of the nation. Nor is he interested in the kind of connoisseurship that is the delight of wine tasters and parodists alike. Perhaps somewhere there are beer pundits in pastel-coloured shirts who sniff their beer, sip it, dreamily roll it round their palates fine, then spit it into a receptacle intended for that purpose before finally pronouncing it to be a good-natured little bitter though rather heavy-handed in the higher registers. Your true beer drinker, by contrast, rightly knocks it straight back without any nonsense – rightly, so it is said, because the tastebuds in charge of registering bitterness are mostly at the back of the tongue. Whatever the reason, beer is for gulping rather than sipping, and appreciation is expressed not in ornate metaphors but by ordering the same again.

This does not mean that your beer man is not interested in the quality of what he's drinking, or that he has nothing to say about it. He is, and he does, and most of what he's saying nowadays is not very complimentary.

In the last week or so I have been talking about beer to a completely representative, sociologically precise cross-section of the community who, by an almost incredible stroke of luck, I happened to bump into in various public houses in London. The most widely expressed complaint was about keg (top-pressure) beer, which was unfavourably compared with the Real Thing which is pumped up by hand from the cellar. Keg beers were accused of being too weak, too gassy and too sweet. When, I was asked rhetorically, did I last taste hops? In how many pubs, I was further challenged, are the pump-handles anything but quaint bits of decor for American tourists to gawp at? A less usual complaint (one person, to be exact) was that pub beer tastes of washing-up liquid: this is not surprising when you see the way some pubs wash their glasses, and is something worth watching out for.

As for the pubs themselves, complaints centred on how the wicked brewers are ripping out landlords and old interiors and replacing them with managers, plastic flowers, soft carpets and piped music. One witty fellow described the process of pub-modernisation as Formication.

But grumbling about beer and pubs is a popular and time-honoured British pastime, and some complaints are better founded than others. Nor would I be giving a fair picture if I were not to mention the bouquets as well as the brickbats. The general availability of draught Guinness in recent years was welcomed, as was the arrival of Newcastle Brown down South. God was thanked by more than one Londoner for Young's brewery. White Shield Worthington received high praise (that's the one that must be poured carefully and steadily in order not to disturb the sediment, which should be left in the bottle).

What was apparent from my rapid survey was the high general level of interest and awareness on the part of beer-drinkers. For many years they have sat on their high stools at the bar in a state of deep lethargy. Doubtless this state was induced by the beer, and perhaps the reason for their new alertness is that the beer isn't doing its job properly. At any rate, they're waking up, they're looking around and drinking their beer, and they're not uncritical of what they're seeing and tasting. It is for such people that this column is intended. It will be concerned not only with beer and brewing, but any other ancillary subject-matter from beer ads to pub games, from hop-picking to licensing laws. I hope it will be a collaborative venture, and very much welcome any information, advice or criticism from readers (including, of course, publicans and sinners – I mean brewers).

Richard Boston, August 11 1973

* * *

The morning after
This is the morning when the stomach passes its verdict on nearly a week of gastronomic judgment. Drink is never a more dangerous delight than in its traditional Christmas season: and the longer the Christmas, the longer and more potentially damaging the delight. Unless drink is handled more coolly than many of us contrive it is likely over a week to create a wound none the less painful for being self-inflicted. The hangover has many aspects, each of which can demand separate treatment. The headache, the cartoonists' simple picture, is relatively easy to treat; aspirin – though rarely in small doses – will relieve it.

Hangover, though, is the cheerful term for alcoholic poisoning which, in its usual relatively mild form, is best treated by rest and warmth. 'Sleeping it off' is no loose term. The enduring and chastening part of a hangover resides in the stomach.

The wise – that enviable minority – take Alka Seltzer, health salts or, at least, copious draughts of water before they go to bed after the party, but once the stomach has acted as host to its enemy all night it needs more powerful relief next morning.

There are many theories about this. The 'hair of the dog' recipe is old but not, as a rule, convincing. The ancient remedy of the beer drinker – bottled Bass – lies cold upon the stomach. Fernet Branca, the patent draught with a high reputation, often will not lie upon the stomach at all. Underberg sometimes proves both soothing and bracing. The old hands favour a large brandy and water, which is at least stimulating. If the attack is not violent, a glass of champagne – in the words of an addict 'So long as you don't enjoy it' – can be helpful.

The most soothing treatment – in conjunction with sleep and comfort – is warm food. There is an originally American publication called *The Hangover Cookbook*, but this is no time for reading books, even if the eye can follow, the brain absorb and the hands execute, its instructions. What is needed is simple, and rapid comfort. For those who can stomach it, porridge affords a gastric blanket. Onion soup may be better; the French package is convenient, better if reinforced by fresh onion; the sophisticated add a slug of brandy. Eggs a la King; or, simpler, scrambled eggs liberally sprinkled with Worcester sauce; kedgeree or fish mush; corned beef hash; shepherd's pie – all these soothe. The difficulty usually is to persuade the sufferer that food is the best cure. If that cannot be done then – although chemically it adds another sugar to the alcohol sugar which is the root of the trouble – hot, strong and sweet tea or coffee will afford some relief.

What of the depressing-looking drinks that remain undrunk? Spirits, sherry and port retain their quality the better if they are kept corked; but, even neglected, they die hard. Table wines are more fragile and, after a couple of days uncorked, a quarter bottleful is not a worthwhile commodity. Wine left-overs, though, are a valuable adjunct to cooking. For culinary convenience and advantage, keep the white wines – of any kind – in one bottle; the red is another. The whites can be mixed. When a recipe asks for 'Chablis or sauternes' the difference between white wines – for cooking purposes – has disappeared. In the case of red wines the better, older bottles, with their sediment, are less useful than the poorer with no residue. Mix them, but filter out the lees before using. White wine adds immensely to a fish dish, red to meat, especially beef. The important factor is that the wine should be added early or after steady boiling: that is to say, the alcohol should have evaporated before the wine becomes part of the dish. A hasty late slop of wine will spoil the flavour and damage digestion. A judicious addition of wine does enhance the odds and ends of the Christmas fowl or joint and – aided by a bottle of ordinaire on the table – makes a soothingly tasty end to a holiday.

John Arlott, December 27 1973

* * *

MIXED FEELINGS

In August I listed some of the unpleasant drinks that are forsworn by members of the St Bride's League of Temperance. A reader suggested that an addition to these should be Coke and mild, which he had witnessed being ordered in a pub. My request for further revolting concoctions ordered in all seriousness in British pubs has elicited an enthusiastic response.

Blackcurrant seems to be the most widespread pollutant, and reports have come in from all over the country of lager and blackcurrant, mild and blackcurrant, and bitter and blackcurrant. Strictly in the interest of pure research I ordered half a pint of the latter in my local the other day. The landlord went white and started shaking, but (stout man that he is) poured out the mixture. It looked like ox-blood, and the one sip I took of it tasted indescribably sweet and sickly. Some people seem to have the idea it must be fun writing this column: let them just try drinking bitter and blackcurrant.

Guinness is one of the most violated of drinks. Black Velvet (Guinness and champagne) has long been popular. Personally I prefer either of the ingredients on its own to both in combination, but champagne is much preferable to the other things that get mixed with Guinness. I came across Guinness and blackcurrant in Liverpool last spring. Now I hear of such horrors as Guinness and lime, Guinness and orange, Guinness and Coke, Guinness and advocaat (oh, my God), Guinness and ginger beer, Guinness and tomato juice, and Guinness and Vimto. In the Wolverhampton area, Vimto is also a popular addition to mild.

From the library of Trinity College, Dublin, comes news of gin-and-milk ordered in all seriousness in a pub in Bishop's Stortford. Assorted other vilenesses: sherry and lime; Pernod and cider (Freddo's Wine Bar, Nottingham); Pernod and Coke (Rose and Crown, Hampton Wick); Pernod, lemonade and blackcurrant (Queen's Arms, Slapton, South Devon); Pernod, lime, blackcurrant and (oh, no) Benedictine; port and Guinness; port and dry ginger; cider and Green Chartreuse; rum and tomato juice.

Apparently the original horrid mixture, Coke and mild, is very popular in Dorset, especially among the fishermen. Dave Arrowsmith tells me that while working as a temporary barman he not only came across Vimto and Guinness but heard a name for it – Pink Velvet. Robin Forrester worked some years ago at the White Horse, Fleet Road, Hampstead, where one customer used to ask for tomato juice and a tablespoonful of Worcester sauce, topped up with draught Guinness.

Bryan Taylor sent me a cutting from *Newsweek* of 12 August about Ernest Hemingway's son, Jack Hemingway, who is aged 50 and whose regular drink is red beer – tomato juice and beer (no wonder the bell tolled). A reader who for some reason wishes to remain anonymous contributes a beautiful piece of observation: 'I could not help hearing a young man emphasising which marque he wanted for his brandy and blackcurrant.'

Mrs Voss of Bristol is not sure if the following counts as a revolting drink but she was in a pub recently when the man next to her ordered a pork pie to eat with his glass of Benedictine. Mr Gareth Chester-Jones of Sheffield tells me he recently served a half pint of Guinness with lime and a splash of lemonade: the next order was for a brandy with port and a dollop of peppermint.

Jim Andrews tells me that in Oldham some 30 years ago, 'when Oldham had as many pubs as days in the year and was known throughout the north as the boozer's paradise', football excursions from Leeds to Barrow would advertise 'stopping in Oldham on the way back', a diversion of about 200 miles. A popular Oldham tipple at that time for those with jaded appetites was champagne and Horlicks with a new-laid egg in it.

Anthony Timaeus was told by Jack Patrick, who kept the Black Lion in New Quay, Cardiganshire (the Llareggub of *Under Milk Wood*), that after closing time he and his cronies used to compete to make the nastiest possible drink from bottles on the shelves: the winner was a mixture of Holland's gin and the juice from a jar of cockles. Mr Timaeus has more recently witnessed in a club in New Quay two parts Southern Comfort, one part dry Martini, ice and lemonade: also one part Pernod, one of gin, one of dry Martini, Schweppes orange, ice, lemonade and two straws.

In order to decide which is the nastiest of all these, I would have to try them all out, which I have no intention of doing. It's bad enough just writing about them: you've no idea how difficult it is to type with one hand clapped over your mouth. So there are no prizes, I'm afraid, but many thanks to all who contributed and I'm sending a fiver to the Council for the Preservation of Rural England.

Richard Boston, November 9 1974

* * *

GUARDIAN SPIRIT

Deep in the cellars under Gray's Inn Road, between Richard Boston's pad and the directors' brandy vault, is the drink-dossier of the *Guardian* reader. It is maintained by a lady who laboured in and out of licensing hours to establish his/her tastes, choices and habits in liquor.

Sometimes, of course, he/she is teetotal – but only to the quiet turn of 18 per cent – 7 per cent less than the national average. More than half of the 858,000 readers who drink – 458,000 – do so twice or three times a week; a quarter of them daily.

Two-thirds of all readers drink bottled beer, lager or stout; a half (considerable overlap here) draught, and a half canned, beer. Three-quarters take sherry, a half vermouth, and a third port. Over a quarter drink in pubs once a week or more – almost a fifth above the national figure.

Some 707,000 drink table wine; that is 56 per cent of the entire readership, compared to 43 per cent of the adult British population. *Guardian* readers, however, double the national figures in that more than half drink wine in their own homes; a third in other people's homes; and a quarter on holiday abroad. Half of them drink wine in restaurants.

What wines do they drink? Rosé is clearly ahead: 32 per cent sometimes drink it, and it also has the highest solus figure of those who, when they drink wine, always drink rosé.

It is not possible to identify precisely which kinds of these wines they choose, except where figures are available for specific trade name brands which many serious wine drinkers hardly ever drink. The figures for branded table wines, however, are just what one would expect. Mateus Rosé is well in the lead – 31 per cent (all but 1 per cent of all those drinking rosé) sometimes drink it – followed by Hirondelle (16 per cent), Blue Nun (12 per cent), Corrida (11 per cent), and Don Cortez (9 per cent).

Among other aperitifs, a third of *Guardian* readers drink Martini, a fifth Cinzano, a sixth Dubonnet and an eighth Pernod.

The most popular spirit is whisky – over half drink it at times; it is followed by liqueurs (45 per cent), and brandy (44 per cent). More than a third drink rum (24 per cent Bacardi) and gin, and 28 per cent drink vodka.

More than a half at some time drink cider (10 per cent rough or draught); one third British sherry, port, or wine.

John Arlott, March 13 1975

* * *

A SLIPPER OF CENTILITRES

In 1973 M Michel Poniatowski, then Minister of Health, tried to persuade the French to stop drinking calvados for breakfast. At the time most Frenchmen drank after breakfast too, averaging a litre of wine a day. However three million Frenchmen drank more than that and a thirsty million drank two litres daily. Hardly any of them listened to M Poniatowski. Having ignored the Minister of Health in 1973 will they now listen to cautionary voices from the drink trade of all people. Seven glasses a day is enough, say the chairmen of Cointreau, Noilly-Prat, Hennessy, Picon, Pernod-Ricard, Remy Martin, Benedictine, and St Raphael; amazingly.

The validity of the proposition that your eighth drink is bad for you depends, of course, on the size of the container in which you put it. Eight slipperfuls of champagne might be inside the limit (unless the lady has large feet) whereas four tumblerfuls of gin would be excessive. The chairmen, united as the Institute for Scientific, Economic, and Social Research into Drink, admit that their measurements are rough and ready but say that if you drink from the container, normally held to be appropriate to the stuff you are drinking, seven glasses is seven centilitres of alcohol and seven centilitres is all right. According to a poll by the Institute, however, 40 per cent of Frenchmen and 8 per cent of Frenchwomen over 18 disagree with this. Statistics prove that for them seven centilitres is not enough and that a million two-litre men think it is not nearly enough.

On the other hand the Institute's assessment of how much booze is good for you is a lot higher than that of Dr Francis Anstie and the US Health Department. In 1864 Dr Anstie concluded that 4.2 centilitres a day (in his Scottish way he called them one and half fluid ounces) was the safe limit which (again in his Scottish way) he defined as three and a half whiskies. After extensive trials and experiments last year in Framingham, Mass., and Alameda County, Cal., the Health Department announced that Dr Anstie was absolutely right and that 4.2 centilitres might even improve your life expectancy. Perhaps it would have been too much to expect that a limit expressed in terms of whisky would commend itself to Cointreau, Noilly-Prat, Hennessy, Picon, Pernod-Ricard, Remy Martin, Benedictine, and St Raphael.

May 17 1975

* * *

BROKEN CLASSES

In the last decade wine drinking in Britain seemed to have spread across most class and financial barriers. Now the trade doubts if that is the case. It appears that the post-war increase was already losing momentum when the duty increase imposed by the last Budget virtually halted it.

In 1974, wine imports increased by only five per cent compared with 26 per cent in 1973. That increase cancelled itself out since the per capita sale remained the same, at nine bottles a year. In the United States, where consumption has doubled in 13 years, the figure is also nine bottles a year; but this is an average from uneven returns. In Washington, the estimate is 25 bottles per head: in California 20: in Alabama, one.

In Britain the five main wine buying groups are separated predominantly by class divisions. The first is that of people born into families where a wine cellar had been maintained for generations. Formerly they took price rises in their stride; now many of them are looking for cheaper wines in their habitual kinds. Then comes the large alcohol-per-penny sector which accounts for a considerable proportion not only of cheap imported wine, but was probably responsible for last year's 143 per cent increase – more than twice as high as that of all imported wines – in sales of British wines. Luxury drinking in restaurants, hotels, and night clubs is beginning to show some decline, which is probably due to the exaggerated mark-ups many of the same restaurants are already beginning to regret. The immigrant element of people from wine producing countries may be relatively small, but it treats wine as an essential item of living and, although hit by the budget increase, it will continue to buy wine. Celebratory drinking has declined less in volume than in expenditure. The 21st, wedding, christening, or anniversary party-giver is demanding lower prices which caterers are hard pressed to meet.

Finally there is the considerable section of post-war converts to wine. Led to it by war service, travel, holidays or simply local fashion, these buyers are now under financial pressure, but they will be forgoing more than drink if they cannot continue to buy wine. These, in the fashion of the British and the Americans, but not the people of the tradition of wine producing countries, have made wine a hobby. Generally middle, or lower-middle class, they represent the significant growth in British wine consumption in the past couple of decades. They are the missionary sector the trade cannot afford to lose. They have also caused the increase in the publication of wine books, the sale of wine artifacts, the production of wine films, and the proliferation of wine merchants during the past decade.

They are the people who talk and read about wine, who form appreciation societies and tasting groups. They are the people for whom such books as *Princes of the Grape* (Weidenfeld and Nicholson, £4.50) are published. Written by Anthony Rhodes, it is an anecdotal history of the great wine makers, from as far back as Ausonius in St Emilion and Horace in Tivoli; the Champagne widows, Ingham and Woodhouse in Marsala, the Spanish sherry barons, the wine nobility of 18th-century Bordeaux; the English in Oporto, the aristocrats of Germany, the Baron Ricasoli in Italy.

It is the product of much travel in the vineyards and reading about them, and it will prompt many to further reading on these themes, and to discussion – especially of the surprisingly large part played by the British in such matters.

John Arlott, June 26 1975

* * *

Boston on Thatcher on beer

My cat leaves the room when Mrs Thatcher appears on television but, as on the subject of eating sparrows in the bedroom, I take a different line. I find Mrs T quite fascinating, and what I like best is the way she adopts that schoolteacher's tone of Now-listen-very-carefully-because-I'm-going-to-say-this-once-and-once-only and then proceeds to say it seven times. It's even better when she says the opposite of what she means. Small businesses, she told her admirers at the seaside last week, have been the victims of a particularly disastrous vendetta by the Government. She must surely mean that they have been the victims of a particularly successful vendetta. I claim no expert knowledge on the subject of vendetta, but wouldn't a disastrous one be a vendetta in which everything was being bungled and no one ended up being hurt, which is after all the purpose of the enterprise?

In the same speech Mrs T said that the Labour Party is like a pub where the mild is running out. If someone didn't do something soon, she said, all that would be left would be bitter and all that was bitter would be Left.

I've tried looking at these remarks from every angle to see if I can make head or tail of them I've even tried reading them backwards – 'Left be would bitter was that all and.' I foolishly tried them out on my new semantiscope, thereby shattering the wretched instrument into a thousand pieces.

Let us take the sentences one at a time. 'The Labour Party is like a pub where the mild is running out.' My dear

Mrs Thatcher, the whole country is like a pub where the mild is running out. Mild has dropped from 42 per cent of the beer market in 1959 to less that 14 per cent in 1973 and is still declining. If I've said that once I've said it a dozen times. I'm beginning to think that some of you at the back haven't been paying attention.

Mrs Thatcher then said that if someone didn't do something soon, all that would be left would be bitter. It sounds like a very funny pub. No lager, no Guinness, no White Shield, no whisky, no rum, no sherry, no port, no soda-water. Decidedly odd, but not as peculiar as her next statement. 'And all that is bitter will be Left.' Many languages attribute gender to inanimate objects, and most native English speakers find it a little amusing that the French and Italians and Germans have to decide whether a mild-bottle, or a parsnip, or a pneumatic drill, or a prune, is male or female. But in no language, so far as I am aware, are inanimate objects supposed to have political opinions.

That Mrs Thatcher should think bitter or any other kind of beer is left-wing is especially strange since the brewers are Tories to a man and among the biggest contributors to her party's funds. Did not Winston Churchill call the Tory party a brewer's dray blocking the road of progress? He did. Did not Mr Heath call beer a Conservative drink? No, he did not.

I suppose that if bitter is Left, then gin-and-tonic is Right. Wincarnis is obviously moderate. But what about Worcestershire sauce? Or milk? Or lager-and-blackcurrant juice? Wait a bit, perhaps she has a point after all. Lager-and-blackcurrant juice could well be the dangerous political conspiracy which is sapping the very fabric of society as we know it.

Richard Boston, October 18 1975

* * *

THESE MEN ARE DANGEROUS

One of the most dangerous groups of criminals in the country will be more busy than usual today. By tonight they will probably have killed 10 people. In a normal year they cause at least 2,500 deaths and leave many thousands more injured. Yet yesterday spokesmen for the British Medical Association and the AA both opposed stricter police measures to combat the criminals. Fortunately both associations are likely to be over-ruled by the Government, which is expected to publish the Blennerhassett report on drinking and driving this week. As long ago as last summer the Minister of Transport, John Gilberts, was talking about the need for a crackdown on drunken driving. Backed by Blennerhassett, Dr Gilbert should succeed; but it is not going to be an easy task.

Drunken drivers benefit in Britain from our society's grossly distorted double-standards. To be sent to prison for being a drunken down-and-out will not cause a whimper of public protest, but imprisonment for drunken driving is still regarded by many people as unfair.

One reason why the British drunken driver receives such widespread sympathy is because so many people get away with breaking the law. The obvious way to correct this defect is to improve enforcement. An added bonus is that detection is always a better deterrent than prison. Detection of drunken drivers is not a difficult task. By far the biggest proportion commit their crimes on their way home from clubs or pub. Yet under the present procedure the police are reluctant to carry out random breathalyser tests because of the uproar this idea caused when Mrs Castle first proposed it. Indeed, as a concession to the opponents of her 1967 Act, Mrs Castle agreed that the police should not give random tests. (Theoretically, there is nothing to stop random tests now – the Act allows the police to stop drivers where there is a 'reasonable cause' to believe the driver is over the limit – but in practice the police have deferred to the drink lobby.)

All manner of arguments will be raised by the motoring lobby against random tests. The unfortunate AA spokesman yesterday scratched around for three unconvincing and illogical arguments. First, that because some police forces were short of men, this would reduce both the number of random tests and their deterrent effect (which overlooks the police forces which are not short of manpower, and concedes the major point that random tests do deter drunken drivers). Second, that they would waste the police and motorists' time (which in the case of the police, who would catch more drunken drivers, is simply not true and in terms of motorists the waste would be minimal – it doesn't take long to breathe on silica crystals). Third, that they would divert the police from dealing with offenders (which is also untrue as many offenders would be caught by random tests). At present the police usually wait until a traffic offence has been committed or an accident occurred before requiring a motorist to submit to a breathalyser test. This is a daft system. You don't wait until the bomb has gone off if you see a suspected terrorist carrying a dangerous looking parcel. The sooner the Government authorises random tests, the better.

Leader, April 19 1976

* * *

LIQUID LUNCHES BREED LASSITUDE

As the office afternoon wears on you may find your eyelids slowly drooping, your concentration vanishing and your mistakes multiplying. A common enough office worker's malaise – and it may all be the fault of the cheese roll and gin and tonic you gulped down in lieu of lunch.

A study published by the British Nutrition Foundation in its latest *Nutrition Bulletin* contains alarming news for all those given to indulging in the liquid lunch.

Professor Vincent Marks of Surrey University has discovered that the average businessman's lunch-time drinks, accompanied by carbohydrates, produces hypoglycaemia – abnormal reduction of sugar content in the blood – or, as it is more usually known, falling asleep at one's desk.

It has been known for nearly 40 years that alcoholic drinks can cause this condition in undernourished and fasting people. But recent evidence has shown it can be induced after only moderate drinking by healthy people – and that trying to soak up the alcohol with a sandwich only makes things worse.

Volunteers in the Surrey experiments were induced to drink gin and tonic, gin and slimline, or tonic alone, but blood glucose fell to lower levels after the gin and tonic than after the other two drinks. The volunteers consumed the equivalent of about three double gin and tonics which, say the researchers, is well within the amount consumed by some businessmen and others accustomed to bar stool lunches.

Less affluent pub lunchers may more commonly partake of a few pints of beer but there is little cheer for them. A mixture of beer and sandwiches produces almost the same amount of alcohol and glucose as the gin meals consumed by the volunteers.

The symptoms of hypoglycaemia do not appear, however, until several hours after lunch. Consequently, says the report, the late afternoon hazards of undue fatigue, lack of concentration, errors of judgement – or even headaches, inner trembling and feelings of anxiety – may fail to be attributed to their real cause.

Melanie Phillips, January 17 1978

* * *

IT'S TIME WE STOPPED NEGLECTING THE HAZARDS OF DRINK

'Drunken people are a figure of fun to so many but it isn't funny trying to heave 12 stone of prostrate husband off the main road before a container lorry puts an end to his misery.'
Mrs KMM, Cambridge

Drunks are not a figure of fun for me – they are among the most deeply boring people on earth, because they are so utterly predictable. I remember a friend with, thank heavens, many other saving graces, whose behaviour after four whiskies was always exactly the same: six verses of Green Grow the Rushes O, one chorus of Knocked 'Em in the Old Kent Road, a short burst of tears as he recalled his ghastly mother and crash, he hit the floor for the rest of the evening. Even under the panic and fear aroused by violent drunks lies the yawning chasm of boredom – he'll break three dishes, boot the cat across the floor, swear at me for five minutes and then start hitting me.

In wives, drunks may arouse some sympathy; in children, very little but fear and hate. One girl told me how she came home from school one day, opened the front door and saw down the corridor the swinging feet of her alcoholic father, hanged. 'Oh I felt so happy,' she said, 'I went belting down the road to find my mother and tell her we were all right now.'

At age 20 I discovered I could drink strong men under the table and never turn a carefully back-combed hair. It was then that I first rejected the idea of male superiority – it is extremely difficult to feel inferior when you are merrily compos mentis and your male companion has stretched his snoring length upon the floor. But that in itself says a lot about our general attitude to alcohol. Drink was a test of manhood, the man who couldn't carry his drink was to be despised and I, who could, was full of empty pride. No wonder the attempt to down a lot of fermented liquid is one of the first initiation rites of male adolescents and no wonder many parents smile secretly to themselves at their young son's staggers, however much they may upbraid him in public.

Of course we all know and deplore the effect alcohol can have on some, but then, we argue, all good things can be abused and turned from a blessing to a cross. Moderation is the key and if some do not practise moderation, then they must pay the penalty and expect us, the moderate, to deprive ourselves of a seemly pleasure. And yet, in a decade that has put governmental health warnings on cigarettes and is about to make seat belts compulsory, drink hazards seem oddly neglected. No-one ever battered the living daylights out of their wives and kids, caused another's death, went to prison or lost job after job through being a two-pack a day man or forgetting to fasten a seat belt. Evidently we are blind to the problems of drink.

But a new report from the Royal College of Psychiatrists, published today (Tavistock Publications, £1.95), could open our eyes. The statistics on the effects of drink and drink-related offences, not to mention the millions of pounds that alcohol's misuse costs us, are staggering in themselves and rising all the time. The report emphasises that, without any scaremongering, we already have cause for serious concern and if adolescents continue to drink more (as they are), women join men in consumption (as we are) and we all join the Frenchmen's levels in the boozy Common market, then the future poses 'threats which are potentially appalling'.

The report suggests, among other things, that governments should shoulder their responsibilities and think very carefully before they ease licensing laws or lower the price of drink (both measures are directly co-related to alcohol consumption).

But it is clear that a change in our own personal attitudes to drink could eventually save us even more. Television playwrights could think of something else for their characters to do when at a loose end than pouring drinks. Owners of companies (as the psychiatrists recommend) could devise ways of lessening their employees' pressure to drink. Parents can teach their children the civilised techniques of drinking. And we ourselves could refrain from pouring drinks down the throats of visitors who have visibly had too much and make sure we always have a good supply of soft drinks to hand.

Jill Tweedie, February 8 1979

CHAPTER NINE
DROWNING
DISCONTENT

THE great British tradition of afternoon pub closing was finally abolished with the passing of the 1988 Licensing Act. Well, almost – public houses and clubs in England and Wales could now serve alcohol from 11am to 11pm every day but the closure on Sundays remained sacrosanct. And, north of the border, the shutdown had already ended with the passing of the Licensing (Scotland) Act of 1976.

Despite pushing through this liberalisation of the law – in the face of some serious opposition from the medical profession – the Conservative party in 1988 was getting worked up about mobs of affluent youths rampaging through country towns. John Patten, a Home Office minister, dubbed this 'the Saturday night lager culture' and its associated 'lager louts'. Thus a cliche was born and within days newspapers had adopted it to describe any kind of alcohol-related trouble – including Viscount Linley, who sued the *Today* newspaper when it labelled him an upper-class lager lout.

Whether the consumption of lager led directly to greater levels of loutism was debatable. Young people had been drinking and causing trouble for over a century, while the infamous 1980s football hooligan 'firms' rarely touched the stuff as it impaired their fighting ability.

Lager consumption greatly increased during the decade but it wasn't just pints of the fizzy stuff that was selling but a wide variety of bottled beer. In part this was due to the appearance of fridges in bars but was also because consumers were becoming much more conscious of brands. Swigging exotic-sounding beers from around the world became the fashion – from the latest German pils to Mexican beer with a piece of lime rammed down the bottleneck. Canned beers were also taking off and in 1989, Guinness launched the widget, a pressurised plastic device that produced a creamy head from the can.

In response to some serious alcohol abuse Britain's leading drinks companies united to form the Portman Group, to suggest initiatives to reduce burdens associated with excessive drinking. One of the first was an ID card for 18-year olds to reduce underage drinking although it took a few years for the idea to be adopted.

A strong case could be made for calling the 1980s the decade of the restaurant. The wine bars that had appeared in the 1970s were turning into French-style brasseries, and even pubs were beginning to offer a little more than sandwiches and crisps. After years of neglect pubs began to refurbished although drinkers were often shocked to discover that their local had been turned into a theme pub complete with a new name such as the Slug and Lettuce. There were disco pubs, sports bars, American diners and the ubiquitous Victorian-style pub. Wine drinking was on the increase with consumption reaching a new high of an average of 12.4 litres per person, although to put this in perspective the French were drinking an average of 74 litres per head.

John Arlott's consumption was probably more than the latter figure, but after 12 years or so of giving expert advice on all matters wine, he retired in 1980. It would seem though that not everyone at the *Guardian* had been reading his columns. At his leaving party in the paper's boardroom, he was reported to have commented 'I fear the worst' after glancing down at a table covered in plastic wine glasses and cheap, warm plonk. The quality of wine at *Guardian* events has greatly improved since then, particularly from the mid-1990s.

* * *

PERMISSION TO DRINK, SIR

There used to be a nasty tradition in all British armed forces stationed abroad of making leave conditional on surviving a course of cautionary lectures and films. Before any squaddie, erk, or matelot was allowed a week away from his unit to swing a loose leg along the streets of Cairo or Alexandria, Calcutta or Cox's Bazaar, he was compelled to undergo a couple of days' intensive brainwashing which included a security officer on the dangers of leaking vital military information, which very few had, a padre on avoiding the moral dangers almost all were praying they would immediately run into, and a medical officer on the dangers of VD, illustrated by a couple of X-certificate films in horrifying Technicolor.

I have never actually met, though I often heard tell of, men who were so affected that they tore up their passes and asked permission to stay behind and help out in the orderly room. It is certainly true that for tens of thousands, the first day or so was blighted by that awful chorus of warning voices ricocheting around in their heads.

Every year the pre-Christmas weeks remind me more and more of those pre-leave days. On every hand there is a voice or a pen lifted to promise dreadful consequences for those who indulge in the customary rites of the season: watch the calories, watch the cholesterol count, watch that the children's toys don't cut his knee or warp his mind, watch you don't get pregnant at the office party, or raped while carol singing. And every and anon like an insistent refrain to all the other many and varied cautions, warnings about the dangers of strong drink.

The anti-drink forces are, of course, active all through the year, producing, it sometimes seems, a new report every week. That is no doubt fair enough since the brewers and distillers advertise all year round. Christmas, however, sees both groups mounting their maximum effort – the one hoping to reach everyone, even including maiden aunts who only have a sherry or ginger wine at Christmas, the other hoping much the same but to get in first.

If all this sounds as though it is going to develop into an attack on the anti-alcohol brigade and arguments in favour of uninhibited, unrestricted drinking at Christmas, or any other time, let me pause at once and say it is nothing of the kind. What it is is a very small plea, uttered in a very soft voice, for a less universally negative note in all the warnings and cautions. By all means let the occasions when it is foolish or criminal to drink be emphasised, but couldn't we also hear a word from the same side of the fence about when it is safe and possibly even desirable to take a glass or two?

Plainly no one needs telling about alcohol as a social lubricant at parties and other social gatherings. But there are less obvious occasions and situations where it can work fruitfully. A man I know is very fond of poetry and likes to read it aloud. Stone cold sober he finds this difficult to do, but half a bottle of wine makes all the difference. Some of his pleasantest evenings are spent sitting with a book in his hand and some wine at his elbow declaiming Wordsworth and Tennyson to an empty room.

Most people who cannot sing, sing better with a drop or two inside – or if they don't sing better, they think they do, which is just as pleasurable. Singing and drinking tend to evoke pictures of drunks supporting themselves on lamp-posts, while intoning Nellie Dean in a tuneless drawl. It can be otherwise. There are friends who make music at home and enjoy wine with it. There are sessions around pub pianos with beer liberally drunk but ending quite safely and near soberly at closing time.

My own personal preference – and one which I intend to indulge fully this Christmas – is for drinking while cooking. I find they go together remarkably well, though best if you put off the first glass until everything is prepared and in position. Then you can sip away while stirring and tasting and titivating the meat. There is always something on hand to nibble, and with an open bottle beside you, you will never be entirely without company in the kitchen.

Other people will no doubt have their own favourite combinations, and it is up to all at this season to share experiences and to recommend the good ones to the uninitiated. After all, the reason so many squaddies ended up in the Grant Road, Bombay, or the Berka in Cairo, was that these were the only places of pleasure they had ever heard mentioned.

Harry Whewell, December 19 1980

* * *

NO PICK UP FOR THIS PENGUIN

The world's most exclusive – and least drunk – real ale has run dry because its master brewers failed in their efforts to wean the British Army away from gassy beer. Penguin

Ale's makers announced yesterday that they had ceased trading, abandoning a three-year, £170,000 struggle to stabilise a business run from a converted shed on Port Stanley waterfront.

The Penguin Brewery began with the pedigree of Everards of Leicester behind it and a potential clientele of 5,000 residents and troops in the British garrison on the Falkland Islands. It opened in an amber flush of evangelism in early 1983, only months after the conflict ended.

An Everards executive, Ron Barclay, brought brewing tanks to a place where draught beer had never been tasted before. He spent two months matching the malt to the local water and palates – but made some unwelcome discoveries. Port Stanley's four public houses always have sold canned or bottled beer because draught does not travel well by sea. So they have no cellars. The plastic pins of Penguin had to sit on or behind the bars, in pubs which are kept well heated. Unsurprisingly, one publican said yesterday, the ale 'went off rather quickly'.

Although an excellent light-bodied beer, it was unable in its crucial market to dislodge the obsession of British squaddies overseas with canned McEwans, Newcastle Brown and Carlsberg. It was tried in garrison messes but never went down well. At peak output Penguin produced only 1,200 pints a week. Its sales last Christmas were 'disastrous'.

Naafi's assistant secretary manager, Dougie Pullen, said yesterday: 'I'm sorry to hear the venture has gone down. Canned beer is what our customers are used to. It's something they can pick up wherever they go in the world.' Everards said: 'We are disappointed to give up. We think

there is still a business there for local people with the right
energy and ability.'

John Ezard, March 6 1986

* * *

UNTHEMELY BEHAVIOUR

One minute the building was a used car showroom in
Finsbury Park, a few days later, it had turned miraculously
into the White Lion of Mortimer, to all intents and
purposes a well-established old pub – complete with a
grand gold-lettered sign, frosted glass windows and
drinkers propping up the bar. A Victorian pub which comes
in a box, to be erected overnight? Clearly a fake. Or is it?

By chance, my first visit to the ersatz Lion followed
a meal at the Braganza, a smart three-storey restaurant
which has just opened in London's Soho. Although the
latter boasts an airy, art-filled interior, and was designed
by Fitch and Co's Carlos Virgile and Nigel Stone, it felt just
as contrived, and hence uncomfortable, as the pub.
Designers seem to be trapped in their own postmodern
predicament: nothing they create seems to be 'real'.

To most of us, 'theming' smacks of Elvis Presley pubs
and Olde England airport cafeterias. In fact, themes are
often involved when a retailer wishes to reposition a
business for a target market; brewers and leisure chains
have whole menus of themes to choose from. Along with
location, prices, menus, the age and appearance of staff,
interior design signals who a place is for – and to whom,
implicitly, it is out of bounds.

The White Lion, in order to set itself apart as
something more than a bland, mass-produced pub,

offers its working-class customers a generous amount of floor space, real beer, and what the trade calls a 'low Victorian' interior; a mishmash of dark-stained panelling, Christopher Wray-style brass lamps and fans, 'real effect' gas fires in reproduction fireplaces, sub-William Morris wallpaper, and so on.

To this stage set have been added props on shelves symbolically 14 feet above the floor – a bizarre collection of historical icons: odd volumes of a dilapidated Encyclopaedia Britannica, a carriage clock, empty Keiler marmalade jars, a row of saucepans and crockery – plus a one-third-scale model Haywain in prize position above the door. Even without a Barthes-style 'reading' of the assembled objects, you get the message; this is a (William) Morris Minor of pubs, reliable, cosy, social, traditional – but it's also new, which means it is acceptable to the young, the biggest group of new drinkers.

At Bragnaza, in contrast, the very attention to detailing, from low-voltage lighting to parchment-printed menus, shouts 'design' which denotes a particular class of fashion-sensitive customer. Braganza is second-generation Design; conscious that pastiche versions of minimal, high-tech interiors have started to appear in provincial high streets, its designer has recruited Art to give the restaurant added value – of the 'art is unique, so this must be real' variety.

Fraser Taylor, a member of the Cloth fashion design group, has created a big mural which contrasts with a ceiling by the painter, Ricardo Cinalli; its images of ruins and cascading masonry are references to a different, classical, sophisticated past. The fact that, on our visits, both food and service contrived to be tasteless, was no doubt a technical hitch.

More convincing efforts to theme yuppie eateries, such as the Dome brasseries, credit customers with subliminal perception, a sort of sixth sense, with offered-up objects from the past; they make sure the trappings, while artfully contrived, are accurately coordinated. But need they do so? According to postmodern philosophers, who talk of modern life as all-encompassing 'spectacle', we consumers know it's all a game, and enjoy playing it.

Spotting signs, following fashions, comparing one simulation with another, has become a source of pleasure in its own right, they say, because in today's mass culture, among a welter of images and messages, it has become impossible to relate to the real past. In any case, the real past does not correspond to marketing categories, so it has had to be reinvented anyway.

But researchers are nervous about the ability of this postmodern sign-watching to sustain consumer loyalty. 'People resent being bit-players in someone else's play,' says SRU's Jean Carr, 'whether it's about Chicago gangsters, Maigret, or Bugsy Malone. That's why we see the re-invention of the traditional pub, where the theme is domesticity – it demands no performance.'

Mind you, the subtle repositioning of these 'traditional' pubs has mixed blessings; tradition in the image of Richard Branson for example, means the 'Firkin' chain which, while removing the male dominance, excessive drinking and aggression of the old, attracts a homogenised middle-class clientele in their place which is positively inhospitable to, inter alia, pensioners and unemployed people.

'Lifestyle design' disenfranchises the 'non-targeted,' and kills off the old-style street with its volatile mixture of nationalities and classes. The marketeers claim that theming replaces outmoded class barriers; but control of space planning and the imagery therein remains in the hands of those, such as brewers, who have a close resemblance to old-style bosses.

John Thackara, January 8 1987

* * *

APHRODISIAC BEER OFFERS REMEDY FOR SAGGING PROFITS

The ultimate answer to and remedy for brewer's droop could come from a beer bottle, now that a well-known French company has come up with an aphrodisiac brew.

One of the country's oldest breweries, Pecheur et Fischer in Strasbourg, is seeking permission to market a beer low in alcohol with the clear intention of reaching the parts that other beers would not even dare to mention.

Even the label is suggestive: the brew will be sold as 3615 Pecheur. The number is a reference to the minitel phone line used to pick up pornographic dating services on small television sets linked to millions of telephones in French homes and businesses.

The firm's chairman, Mr Michael Debus, said he needed to give his firm's sagging profits a boost because increasing competition from giant European brewers was threatening jobs at his brewery. He was inspired by visits to Africa where his other beers sell well and where he found that Africans were increasingly using plant-based love potions.

'With two of my managers I toured Africa and came back with 32 aphrodisiac plants, ten of which are being used in the beer,' he said. 'I needed 18 months of work but the taste was a bit odd. This has now been disguised by a concoction of hops and mango.'

Mr Debus, who is 62, used himself as guinea pig for the mango-hops cocktail and claimed that regular doses kept him 'in form'. The battle has now started to convince the French Health Ministry that the brew is a real beer and not a medicine.

It had also been decided to keep the alcohol level down to escape stringent French controls on advertising, particularly on television where bottled shandy is the only drink accepted for commercials.

But even if the new brew is given the go-ahead, Mr Debus has warned that the Casanova effect is strictly limited to four bottles a day. After that, 3615 was more of a soporific.

Paul Webster, August 1 1988

* * *

A LONG DRINK THIS SUMMER

In a fortnight you'll be able to drink all day. For the first time since the first world war, pubs will be able to stay open from 11am to 11pm, except on Sundays. Will our city centres and rural towns begin to look like Stuttgart and Dusseldorf after a bad English soccer show? If the experience of Scotland is any guide, such fears are unfounded. The change only brings England and Wales into line with what has been common practice in all continental countries. People who want a drink – and the vast majority do drink sensibly – will find life has become marginally more civilised. Restaurants, pizza bars and bistros will now be able to serve drinks after 3pm.

A minority of drinkers do have a serious alcohol abuse problem. There are also strong links between certain categories of crime and alcohol. Nine out of 10 public order offences – fighting and assaults – are drink-related. But as Douglas Hurd emphasised yesterday, both the police and the magistrates already have extensive powers. In a circular to the two organisations, the Home Secretary reminds them of these existing powers, plus new controls under the 1988 Licensing Act. He is particularly concerned about illegal under-age drinking. Hooliganism and drink are closely related. Publicans will no longer be able to defend their widespread practice of serving under-18-year-olds with the plea that they did not know. The new law places them under an obligation to find out. Meanwhile, neighbourhoods which are troubled by a noisy pub have a new remedy: applications for the revocation of a licence can be made at any licensing session. Under the old procedure revocation was only possible on the date of annual renewal.

Some rural towns – and urban centres – which have been troubled by young people and drink may want to do more. A new by-law in Coventry could be the solution. It stems from complaints of the Chamber of Commerce that youths drinking from beer cans in the centre were offending visitors and fuelling crime. The by-law will prohibit drinking in public squares, parks and streets within the city's inner city ring. In other areas – such as Brighton – close cooperation between police, licensees and brewers has helped cut arrests for alcohol-related disorder by 14 per cent.

In the international consumption league, the UK is well down: 19 states consume more per head of population. A growing proportion here – about 15 per cent – abstain completely. Only two per cent of the population are estimated to suffer from problem drinking. The people best able to control such abuse are the people behind the bar. Now that pubs are open for longer hours, publicans should be more ready to say 'no' to customers who have had enough.

Leader, August 6 1988

* * *

WHY DO LAGER LOUTS GO MOONING?

All summer I've been fascinated by lager louts. They've been mooning at me from almost every tabloid newspaper I've picked up. They've been up north, some have said that they were at Hillsborough on that fateful day. They've been down south, disturbing rural tranquillity, fighting on the village greens.

The pieces I've read about the lager louts have, however, left a lot to be desired. I could discern that violence was part of their culture, and beer, but what was the symbolic significance of mooning? Why did they do it? What did it mean? And what were lager louts in previous incarnations – punks? Yuppies? Skinheads? Young Conservatives?

I needed to find some lager louts to answer these questions. I started in the way that I usually do – I asked my friends and acquaintances. Some of my acquaintances are not averse to the odd spot of violence, some of them are rather loud, some have even mooned – inadvertently, of course. Some even drink lager.

But none of my acquaintances admitted to being a lager lout. I tried them with the dictionary definition of lout and the binding logic to go with it. 'Look, if you can be considered "coarse, ill-mannered fellows" – by anyone, mind – and you drink lager, you're a lager lout.' But they could see through this argument a mile off. 'I may be a lout,' said one, 'but not a lager lout. I'm more a lager-drinking lout, or a lout with a fondness for strong beer, including continental lager. Lager louts are more your contemporary figure like Yuppies or bimbos, aren't they? I've got a girlfriend who's blonde and a bit thick but she's not a bimbo because she's a bit old-fashioned – in fact she seems a bit of a rum-and-blackcurrant lout if you ask me. If birds count, that is.'

I said that they might have to, and that I'd be in touch. But I had one card up my sleeve. I went out looking for George.

I found him, predictably enough, at two o'clock in the morning in a 'niteclub', his customary pint of lager in his hand. What George doesn't know about lager, or the people that drink it, isn't worth knowing. I told him about my quest. 'Lager louts? You're looking for lager louts about here in Sheffield's top nitespot? What's the matter with you? Get yourself off down to Rotherham or try Westminster. There are only VIPs here at this time of night, and the top birds.'

A tall girl with a slightly vacant expression and an ill-fitting blouse greeted him. George showed great lager lout ingenuity. 'Look,' he said, 'my mate and I are shooting a documentary about lager louts. We need a top bird to present the programme. We're looking for a bird like Angela Rippon but without any clothes on. You'd do, just, are you game?' She stared at me with an unconcealed look of disgust. 'Have you put George up to this?' she asked. She glanced at the half of lager in my hand. 'Men are all the same.'

George got down to business. 'Look, let's start with the basics. Where do lager louts like to find themselves after a good night on the piss?' 'The toilet?' I suggested helpfully. George looked at me in a way not dissimilar to the girl with the vacant expression. 'Look, I'll make it easier for you. After 10 pints of lager, what do you really need?' He looked at me expectantly. My eyes lifted heavenwards. George nudged me. 'Come on, think. What do you think that they really want?' 'Well, it's not a toilet,' I said. George nodded. I assumed that George was playing some kind of sophisticated game. 'A catheter?' I suggested at last.

George swore very loudly. 'I can understand why some of these lager louts stick the nut on people sometimes. No, not a bloody catheter – a nice fat kebab, a big juicy curry. Haven't you ever been out before? Haven't you lived? It just so happens that I know this bird who used to work in a curry house. She had to leave in the end because she was getting a bit of stick. She's Chinese, you see, and the blokes ribbed her because of it. You'd probably call these blokes lager louts today, because they'd had a skinful before they went for their curry. She used to tell me about these blokes pissing under the table when she was serving them. They sound just up your street.'

'Indeed they do,' I said as I got my notebook out. 'Urinated under the table, did they? Was there any mooning to go with it? Was there any symbolic display attached to the urinating, or was it purely functional?'

George ignored me, but borrowed a lipstick off the girl with the vacant expression and drew the number of the Chinese girl on the back of a VIP pass. 'Give her a ring. Tell her that you're a friend of George, and don't ask her any daft questions. Tell her you're doing a survey of restaurants for that free paper they stick through the doors. She'll talk to you then.'

A rather meek-sounding voice answered the phone. I felt I couldn't lie to such a trusting voice. I explained the real purpose of why I wanted to interview her. It may have been my imagination, but the gaps between the 'mm-hmms' and the 'yeahs' seemed to be getting longer and longer after I'd explained this to her. I told her I would ring her the following day to arrange the time of the interview.

I was over the moon. This was going to be real hard-nosed journalism. I was going to carry out a first-hand analysis of lager louts in action.

I decided to get into the mood by spending the next night in a bar, ordering pint after pint of the amber nectar. I tried to put myself in their shoes, to see things from their perspective. I seemed to be succeeding. I almost accidentally mooned when I emerged from the toilet without properly fastening my jeans.

I rang Susie when I got home. It was only 11.45pm, but Susie appeared to have been asleep. See what having to deal with those people all the time can do to you, I thought to myself. 'Now, about tomorrow night, Susie, let's run through a few things. What's it like to have urine splashing all over your feet? What do you actually say to someone who moons at you from a few feet away? I'm really going to nail these guys. You know, I'm really on your side.' Susie hung up on me.

I rang the following morning. Susie unfortunately had changed her mind about the interview. 'They were horrible times. I don't want to talk about it.' 'But,' I protested, 'you can't do this. How are we ever going to understand these lager louts if we don't get information about them?' 'Don't worry,' said Susie, 'I already understand them. I just want to forget about them.' 'But what about the headlines?'

My pleading was bubbling to the surface as poorly concealed anger. I realised that I was shouting. Susie hung up on me again. My head slumped forwards. Observers might have described this as headbutting the wall in frustration. I rang George.

'Don't panic,' said George. 'She'll change her mind in a few days. In the meantime, you and I could take a little trip to find some of these lager louts. I feel like a break. You decide where you want to go and I'll be your guide – for expenses, for the beer and that.'

I pulled a map of Great Britain out of the drawer, and a pin. The pin, like the glass on a Ouija board, floated across Liverpool and Manchester then drifted somewhat mysteriously out to the North Sea. It seemed to hover off the coast. I could hear a strangely familiar voice in my head. It was just the odd fragment. Where was I going to find men 'as hard as shite'? Familiar pictures filled my mind. Where was I going to find men with T-shirts who could talk like this without laughing?

Some people would say that Harry Enfield has a lot to answer for. The pin moved mysteriously back to dry land again, and landed smack bang in the middle of Newcastle. George sat his can of lager down right in the centre of the map, leaving a damp ring. 'Just the job,' said George.

The train journey was uneventful, or as uneventful as a day out with George could ever be. He insisted on offering his opinions on the contents of other people's newspapers to the people who were reading them. I was tired before we even got there. We spent the night ambulance-chasing in Newcastle – on foot. Our informants, when we eventually caught up with them, were not that forthcoming: 'We're only trying to have a good time, man.' George insisted on putting the questions to them, and then threatened to stick his nut on to one informant whom he felt was not cooperative.

We got the train back to Sheffield early. George insisted on one last quick bevy when we got back. It was nearly time for last orders and we pushed our way towards the front of the bar. We made it as far as the beer garden at the back clutching our valuable prizes. A gang of mates, huddled in one corner of the beer garden, were running through their repertoire of stories about last year's football season. Their companions were in a huddle some distance off, engaged in girl talk. I couldn't help noticing that all the girls wore white stilettos.

George said it was good to be home: 'The birds in Newcastle are classy, but not as classy as the birds from around here.' The group of men were getting louder and louder. Some of the more expansive gestures now became little playful shoves. One little playful shove caused a lot of beer to be spilt. George was brightening up. 'I think we may see some action around here before the night is out.'

This group now started singing. The landlord asked them to quieten down, and I thought I saw the first tentative approximation to a moon in that one of the gang stuck his bottom out. The girls in their white stilettos seemed to be egging on the prospective mooner.

George told me to get my notebook out. Suddenly he grew agitated. George, it seems, had spotted somebody right in the middle of the group of females – a girl with distinctly Chinese features who appeared to be swapping dirty stories. 'It's Susie, from the curry house.' He started dragging me over towards her. Susie appeared to be fleeing. George refused to believe that she had seen us, and dragged me after her. We pushed through the packed beer garden in hot pursuit.

One of Susie's white stilettos got caught in a grate. But so desperate was she to get away from us that she kept on retreating with the grate attached to one shoe. She was now virtually running, with the grate clanking along behind her. The rest of the clientele of the beer garden scattered at this strange sight. George, still apparently believing that she had not seen us, was shouting after her. He dragged me by my lapel. All I could think of was that most of my lager was tipping out of my glass and splashing all over my shoes.

Susie was running for the refuge of the ladies' toilet. She made it. But George is not the kind of guy who is that easily discouraged, and he started banging on the toilet door. He nudged me, and I had to plead for her to come out. What emerged instead was a 50-year-old woman with a face somewhat reddened with anger.

'Bloody lager louts,' she bellowed in my face.

Geoffrey Beattie, August 24 1989

* * *

THE HITS AND MYTHS OF ADVERTISING

James Joyce wrote that you cannot waken a silken nouse out of a hoarse oar but he had not seen the advertising campaign for Piat d'Or wines. He had not laid eyes on the campaign for Cointreau. He was unaware that Australians don't give a XXXX for anything else but Castlemaine.

Advertising can mythologise as potently as word of mouth. Some products need only the mouth. Chateau Lafite, for example, needs no paid ads; it is simply talked about. No one would give Piat d'Or a second glass were it not for that television advertising, so well cast and photographed as it is. The advertising beautifully beguiles all of us into believing it's what the Frogs quaff, when even the peasants who drive the grapes to the factory go home to better Beaujolais.

Take Cointreau. For decades it was a boring drink. Then along comes sexual dynamite in the shape of a TV commercial pitting insouciant French charm against wide-eyed English innocence and off-licences nationwide are having to beat off the punters with clubs.

Yet what is Cointreau at bottom? Nothing more than an eau-de-vie with orange zest. (I've stood beside a huge copper still in Angers and listened to Max Cointreau explain this disarmingly simple process.) What is Cointreau advertising on television? Pure magic. It is an intoxicating ingredient no distiller can add without the help of the alchemists from design companies, advertising agencies and film houses.

The brewer or distiller or viticulteur of an alcoholic drink merely manufactures the product; it takes label designers, copywriters and film directors to manufacture the image. One without the other is a recipe for nothing.

How so? The process for making wine, say, can be minutely documented. But what about the other half of the business, the image making? Like the simple recipe for vodka, can it be infallibly written up and followed?

The first thing to be said is that whereas the physical manufacturing process cannot fail to produce a drinkable product (without guaranteeing a great one), the image manufacturing process, however proficient its practitioners, guarantees nothing. Planning has entered into the process to an unprecedented degree but it was not a planner who squatted on a suitcase at an Arab airport and wrote on the back of an envelope: 'Heineken refreshes the parts other beers cannot reach.' It was a copywriter, aware only that his brief was to say something original about refreshment and lager.

Heineken's brilliant sentence has alchemised a fizzy, urine-coloured gunge of no particular distinction into a major brand of great distinctiveness. At, of course, no small expense. The backs of envelopes may come cheap but the services of copywriters able to utilise them do not; likewise the skills of the film directors who capture the scripted results of such inexpensively inspired moments. John Lloyd, producer of Blackadder, has recorded his surprise upon learning that 19 episodes of his series were made for the same cost as one British Rail commercial.

However, a drink manufacturer who can guarantee his product will get you drunk, cannot guarantee his advertisements will intoxicate anyone. The recent TV campaign for the sherry producers of Spain illustrates this point to perfection. A beautifully made product, suffering from years of negative imagery, has hired on its behalf what was doubtless thought to be a sexy West End ad agency which in turn hires what it doubtless thought was a sexy Soho film director. They produce incoherent balderdash in the hope that younger drinkers will find sherry hip, rather than believing it to be the preferred refreshment of *Telegraph* readers after a larynx-busting Sunday morning in church.

Why is it so difficult to manufacture the right image for a drink? Why, with so much planning and research, so many committed copywriters and gifted film directors, is success so elusive?

Why for every Heineken are there a hundred Johnny-come-nowheres? Why for every Old Grouse are there a thousand anonymous whiskies? And why for every Mouton Cadet are there dozens of plonks?

The answer, I'm happy to report, is the wild unpredictability of the human race; no researcher can plan for it, no copywriter can prejudge it, no film-maker can guess its mood. It is out of the image manufacturers' control.

The human race rejects superlative drinks because the image is wrong and happily swallows mediocre ones because the image is right. This imbalance will keep the marketing profession, not to mention copywriters, furiously employed for years in as inconclusive a task as that which taxed the minds of mediaeval philosophers as they contemplated their angels on pinheads.

Even if the muse appears waving a preprinted envelope, will she be recognised and embraced? Helpless in the face of human contrariness, marketeers turn, like ancient Roman soothsayers, to viscera. But whose gut feel should be heeded? I've witnessed my leanest, most sublime efforts rubbished by a putative marketing genius (Ernest Saunders when he was at Guinness) and I've seen my flabbiest work enthused over by a marketing billionaire (Edgar Bronfman of Seagrams).

In 27 years I have written ads for red, white and rosé wines, apertifs, digestifs, stouts, ales, draught lagers, bottled lagers, draught bitters, whiskies, gins, vodkas, sherries, champagnes, brandies and low-alcohol beers. I've visited scores of breweries, distilleries and vineyards. I've attended dozens of research sessions. All I can say about booze for certain is this: after the digestive system and urinary tract have done their business there is very little difference between any of them.

Malcolm Gluck, March 17 1990

CHAPTER TEN

THIS PLASTERED ISLE

THEY had names like Two Dogs and Moo, came in weird colours and were said to be turning Britain into a nation of teenie-tipplers. Alcopops, mixtures of alcohol and soft drinks, were all the rage in the late 1990s but were felt by some to be targeting 'children hooked on booze', as Frank Dobson, the health secretary, put it in 1997.

The first to appear was Hooper's Hooch, a lemonade-flavoured alcoholic drink launched by Bass in 1995. Many others soon followed, including a whisky-based version of the soft drink Irn-Bru and even alcoholic milk.

There was a media infatuation with alcopops, with all sorts of claims about the evil drinks industry luring children to alcohol. There is no doubt that there were plenty of examples of underage alcopop drinking and juvenile crime cases where the drink was blamed.

Not all though were convinced by the argument that they were deliberately aimed at young children. For a start the drinks were marketed at a premium price, way above the average amount of pocket money. Also, as the drink historian Andrew Barr has suggested, the bright colours and childlike imagery were used 'not in order to appeal to children but in order to reflect the drug-influenced symbols and culture of young people who had already attained legal drinking age'.

Certainly the early part of the 1990s had seen lots of young people abandoning drink in favour of a drug-based rave culture, and alcopops may have been part of a strategy to woo them back. But beer, and specifically lager drinking had never really gone away and from the mid-1990s onwards it was to get a boost by being closely linked with football. Rules about the sponsorship of team shirts had been relaxed and the big brewers were now sponsoring premiership football. At the same time, with the popularity of books such as Nick Hornby's *Fever Pitch*, many closet fans started to come out and admit to enjoying watching the game – often with drink in hand and in front of a wide screen in a pub.

Tastes were changing again with drinkers moving away from bottles and the weaker British brew, or 'cooking lager' as some dubbed it, to premium full-strength lagers such as Stella Artois.

While wine producers didn't go quite as far as to sponsor football matches, the drink was certainly losing its elitist tag. Most of the major supermarket chains were now offering a wide selection of cheap wine. To guide readers to the best of these, the *Guardian* introduced Malcolm Gluck's Superplonk column. Here, the former advertising executive turned wine writer offered advice on the smartest bottles to be found in the supermarket aisles. The long-running column was very successful and led to a number of books of the same name. Wine sales soared, and palates were moving away from sweeter old favourites such as Liebfraumilch to drier ones. Chardonnay enjoyed a massive growth in popularity, with sales no doubt bolstered by the fact that it was the chosen tipple of the fictional diarist Bridget Jones.

For more than 40 years pub design had been through all manner of changes but the only theme that seemed to stand the test of time was some sort of approximation of the traditional English pub. A variation of this was the gastropub, a traditional bar but serving high quality food with a decent wine list and good beer, plus the obligatory blackboard for the menu. The Eagle, just up the road from the *Guardian* in Farringdon, London, was the first to open in 1991 and was much imitated.

Restrictions preventing all-day drinking in pubs, hotels and clubs were swept away in 1995 but the new millennium saw the Labour administration proposing 24-hour drinking. A fierce tabloid-led controversy raged, particularly around the question of binge drinking, but most of the provisions of the Licensing Act of 2003 were supported by the Association of Chief Police Officers. The Act was finally implemented in November 2005, bringing in 24-hour drinking, although few, if any establishments, were truly open around the clock.

Undoubtedly, the early years of the 21st century saw a huge rise in binge drinking, fuelled in part by cheap off-licence sales. Hordes of drunken youths spilled out on to the country's streets each weekend, and violence, vandalism, and the deleterious effects on health were reported on an almost daily basis. But stories of out of control drinkers weren't just confined to the young: there were the middle-aged, drinking themselves stupid in the privacy of their own homes, boozing pensioners, and the overindulging middle classes. There were constant warnings about how many units a man or woman, or even a pregnant woman, should drink, but also confusion over what exactly a unit means. And endless – and contradictory – health reports: one week red wine's good for the body, another it's beer; another, a whisky every night is the key to a long and contented life.

* * *

LINGUA FRANCA: NIGHT ON THE TILES

Now here's a conundrum. What's so manly about getting drunk? What is it about seeing double and talking scribble that proves you're such a mensch? Let's have some sauce and drink this thing over.

Make mine a drop of the hard stuff, a stiff one, straight up, no rocks. Nothing like a few belts to help you get straight, just a couple of shorts and a chaser maybe, not a tankful. Go on, hit me with another shot.

See, getting Brahms and Liszt proves you're a man because it proves you need to lose control sometimes, and if you need to lose control that shows you're mostly in control, like a man's supposed to be.

Say you're down the boozer every night till the last shout, full of gargle and lying about the love life you're always too sloshed to have. That's OK. Or you go on a bender and wake up in Seville with three days' growth and no memory of how you got there. That's a manly tale. Even when you really overdo it, get pissed as a newt and wind up bent double over a Technicolor yawn, it's no big deal.

Some fellas just want to have a good blub, so they get stocious and start talking about something – their kids, the place they grew up – anything that's going to get them crying into their beer. Others are just shy, but they need a few bevvies before they can make conversation. Fine, so long as they're only two-thirds cut, but as a rule they get utterly rat-arsed and repeat themselves all night.

Then there's the ones who are so full of anger they get loaded looking for some peace, but what happens is the cup draws all the anger to the surface. Their faces get meaner with every jar and they suck so hard on their

Marlboros the veins stand out on their necks. And they drink fast, like they can't get the hooch in quick enough. Then that's it, they're ripped and ready to break heads. If you're getting soaked in the same watering hole as fellas like this you're advised not to wear glasses, be black or laugh too loud. It bothers them.

Then again, you could say the purpose of a night on the slurp is not to let your feelings out but the opposite, to get rid of the damn things altogether. To get gone. Bombed. Blitzed.

So here's to us, who's like us, and goodnight. You're away down the street, drunk as a judge (or a lord, or a skunk, or a fiddler's bitch), smashed as a rat, high as a kite, three sheets in the wind, fu' as a puggy (Scots) and feeling great. Maybe you've got a carry out, a little short dog for the road, and you stop on the corner for a pull. You're lit up like a Christmas tree and not a care in the world.

You get home, and you're so far out of your box you can hardly get the key in the door and the stairs up to your flat seem to come at you like a down escalator. You're too soused to get undressed and when you lie down it's the whirling pits and the next thing you're on your knees, talking into the big white telephone, but still you feel good. That is, you don't feel a thing, don't give one damn. That's the whole point, eh? No worries. Cheers!

Stephen Burgen, February 22 1992

* * *

KIDS AND WINE: RITES AND WRONGS

There is an annual celebration in Portugal where people wander round Oporto eating, drinking, singing and tapping each other over the head with plastic hammers. The hammers are a substitute for garlic, traditionally used to ward off illness and evil spirits. They don't hurt (at least, not as much as a string of garlic would) but, after a few hours, you could easily tire of the game. It is a tribute to the equanimity of the Portuguese that no one ever does. The revelry continues long into the night. Now imagine the same festival being held in Britain, complete with punch-ups, pavement pizzas, racist chants and the odd stabbing, and that's if you held it in Surrey.

The countries of the Mediterranean drink a lot more than we do (and, it should be added, have the levels of cirrhosis to prove it), but have produced nothing to compare with the English lager lout. In France, Spain, Italy, Greece and Portugal it is possible for large numbers of people to consume large quantities of alcohol without behaving like something out of *A Clockwork Orange*. Drinking alcohol is still considered a rite of passage in Britain. In the wine-drinking cultures of the Mediterranean, it is seen as an unremarkable, but enjoyable, part of everyday existence. General awareness of alcohol in, say, France is something we could learn from, says Mark Bennett, of Alcohol Concern. In northern Europe, under-age drinking is all about posturing and rebelliousness. Kids want to prove they're adults. But how young should children start drinking alcohol?

According to the Health Education Authority, 89 per cent of boys and girls have had their first proper drink by the time they are 13. Supervision is the key here. You are allowed to give a child alcohol from the age of five in your own home. And it is here that kids should learn to appreciate food and drink in the correct context. You have to be very careful that you don't end up being accused of something terrible, says Peter Duff, of Alcohol in Moderation (AIM), but I don't see the harm in serving watered-down wine to a child of seven or eight. It's important to show a child that wine can be a source of social pleasure, otherwise it tends to be seen as a secret and illicit thing, like smoking. Moderation and parental responsibility are essential. But the more parents can do to take away some of the mystique surrounding alcohol, by introducing it early and in an adult way, the better.

Tim Atkin, July 3 1993

* * *

THEME OF THE WEEK: ALCOPOPS
Worse than spots, worse than puberty, worse than the misery of young love, is the hardship and distress suffered by 13-year-olds desperate to get steaming pissed, but grossed out by the taste of alcohol. Isn't it just typical of the selfishness of adults, with their pints of warm bitter and malt whiskies, to have forgotten how demanding booze is on the young palate? So cheers to the drinks industry for its laudable efforts of late to make the rat-arsed experience more accessible to children. For a year now, the market has been flooded with drinker-friendly 'alcopops' – liquor disguised as fruit drinks and packaged in generationally non-threatening cans.

But the names and images of alcopops are still a little try-hard: Two Dogs, Hooch, Jammin', Rhubarb Rhubarb … trendy, yes, but the suspicion remains that they are not so much authentically young as over-the-hill marketing people's attempts to resonate with the youth vibe.

This week, Carlsberg-Tetley moved a step nearer to getting it right with the launch of Thickhead, a jellified tangerine-flavoured fluid that looks as if it should be stripping rust from the sills of a teenager's Escort, but is, amazingly, designed for human consumption.

Thickhead is as alcoholic as the strongest 'head-banging' lagers, but from the vivid colour and the cheery label, you'd imagine it was a giveaway Sellotaped to the front of the Beano. So misleading is the packaging, with its picture of a tasty young geezer of about 17 pulling a silly face, that the Portman Group, the industry's voluntary regulator, has asked for a redesign.

The name Thickhead, although it does have an appealingly lumpen yobbishness about it along with the implicit promise of a stonking hangover, may be a mistake, but Thickhead is to be welcomed all the same. If Bill Clinton had had it in time, he could have dropped crates of it all over Iraq this week instead of Cruise missiles. The Iraqis would have been misled by the label, too, and drunk Saddam's health with the stuff.

The beverage's name is certain to inspire other new products. Surely it won't be long before an enterprising tobacco company launches a children's cigarette – suggested names: They're Smokin', Life's A Drag, Butthead, or Gemini (it's followed by Cancer).

The relaunched *Punch* magazine could have been a touch more alluring to younger readers had it been given a Thickhead-type name, something more contemporarily violent. Knee in the Groin sounds worthy of consideration.

Jonathan Margolis, September 7 1996

* * *

BEGORRAH OFF

More than privatised railways or Sky Sport, there is one commodity that sums up this free market, New Labour period: the fake Irish pub.

These things have sprouted like weeds in every high street, owned and managed by English breweries, although most decent pubs are already genuinely Irish. It is as daft as if there were chains of Cypriot theme barbers, run by English staff trained to say: 'Do you go anywhere a-nice for 'oliday theece year sir?'

Most real Irish pubs are a delight, with a compulsory lock-in, and a dedicated landlord who's had hardly any contact with life outside his pub since 1964. So the Spice Girls could come in and he'd say: 'Hello girls, I've not seen you in here before, so I've not. I'd be putting some more clothes on if I was you, it's getting cold outside now.'

But the fake ones suddenly appear, all green and yellow with saddles and whips in the window, selling All Ireland Hurling Finals pie and Easter Rising sausage sandwiches. Yet in all the essentials they're the least Irish pubs in the world. Try and get a slightly after-hours drink, and you get the familiar glare which makes you realise no one will ever set up English theme pubs in Kilkenny. Locals would be fascinated as they politely asked for a drink at half a second past eleven – according to the seven minutes fast clock – and were told: 'You've heard the bell, now CLEAR OFF!' Then the windows would be opened as wide as possible and a growling Alsatian released from behind the bar. Let's see if that catches on.

Last Saturday afternoon I was refused entry into an empty O'Neill's because I was with my two-year-old son. Can there be anything in this world more un-Irish than that? I've been in pubs in Dublin where you get funny looks for not having a pushchair.

But question the decision and the nature of these places becomes apparent. 'It's not me, it's a company decision,' you're told. So I rang a series of numbers which led me to O'Neill's centralised customer care department. 'The reason our branches don't have a children's licence,' I was told, is that 'it wouldn't fit the profile and market we aim for with this particular brand.' Then she added: 'We recently reinforced this directive to our managers via email.'

The music, she told me, was centrally chosen as well. Each manager is given tapes to be played at strictly specified points in the day. This must be why you never see a jukebox in O'Neill's. Someone might put on Aretha Franklin during the period in which market research shows the target audience prefers the Kinks. For all we know, focus groups may indicate that this would lead to a 20-minute slump in sales of Cheesy Wotsits.

So even if a member of staff smiles at you, it's probably because they've received an email about the November smiling drive. Just as assembly lines destroy the creativity of factory workers, chains of pubs, hotels and restaurants remove all humanity from their staff and replace it with a soulless corporate friendliness, otherwise described as rudeness. When the lad at a Pizza parlour says: 'Hello, how can I help you with one of our delicious pizzas?' We don't think: 'What a nice chap, eager to help me with one of his delicious pizzas.' Especially if they only teach him the first line, so if you answer: 'I haven't decided yet,' he's likely to say: 'Well hurry up mate, I'm bleeding busy.'

And when you get off an aeroplane to the sound of the poor stewardess repeating: 'Thank you for flying with us, we hope you enjoy your stay,' over and over, it would be much more friendly if they said something human, like, 'Bet you crapped yourself in the turbulence.'

Instead, every member of staff is forced to become a jobsworth, referring each complaint to a faceless, distant code. A variety of rational corporate reasons were given by the customer care woman for why a two-year-old couldn't be allowed in an empty pub for five minutes. But it's like someone in a cafe justifying why you can have bacon and egg, or bacon and beans, but 'we don't do egg and beans'. The only worthwhile response is: 'Can't you see – it's bloody MAD!'

That's why fake Irish pubs fit the New Labour era. They're devoid of all passion, obsessed with ensuring maximum profit, every action is the result of a focus group, and they're ruled entirely from the top with no room for local initiative or dissent.

And it's all presented as innovative and radical. For example, New Labour invites us to enjoy the theme of local democracy, before adding: 'Sorry, you can't bring any Ken Livingstones in here. They don't fit the profile and market we aim for with this particular brand, you see. Anyway, we haven't got a licence.'

Mark Steel, November 18 1998

* * *

Champagne socialists unite: why the left needs Bollinger Bolsheviks

'Where are the *New Statesman*'s priorities?' demands an indignant letter in the magazine's current issue from one Lorraine Hewitt of Whitstable, Kent. She describes the NS's excellent food correspondent, Bee Wilson, and its wine critic, Victoria Moore, as 'intelligent, elegant writers on worthless themes', whose 'trivial, indulgent musings have no place in a journal that is supposed to explore social justice'. Hewitt cannot understand how a leftwing journal allows space for articles on such 'selfish and silly concerns'.

The idea that socialists shouldn't enjoy the pleasures of the table is remarkably hard to dislodge. In the 1930s, Lord Beaverbrook wrote a sneering article for the London *Evening Standard* about 'Cafe Communists', whom he defined as 'the gentlemen, often middle-aged, who gather in fashionable restaurants, and, while they are eating the very fine food that is served in those restaurants and drinking the fine wines of France and Spain, are declaring themselves to be of Left Wing faith.' (One of the Cafe Communists named in the piece replied, with admirable presence of mind, that he didn't see why he should be 'a victim of the malnutrition which is an endemic disease of capitalism'.) When Aneurin Bevan was dining with him, Beaverbrook used to bawl at the butler: 'Bring the

Bollinger Bolshevik a bottle of young, fizzy, cold champagne!'

But, as Lorraine Hewitt demonstrates, it isn't only rich rightwingers who believe that champagne socialism is an oxymoron. The left in this country has its own regiment of puritan zealots who regard any form of fun as a decadent distraction from more urgent tasks.

The late Cyril Ray, a lifelong socialist who edited the *Compleat Imbiber* annuals, had a simple reply to these killjoys: 'There is no more virtue in not minding what you eat and drink than in not minding whom you go to bed with.' Though he refused on principle to allow the *Daily Telegraph* into his house, and once resigned from the *Sunday Times* because of an editorial supporting capital punishment, Ray saw no incongruity in his authorship of a book on Bollinger. As he pointed out: 'They don't say, "How dare you call yourself a socialist and love good books, good painting and good music?" Socialism is about a fuller and richer life for everybody, and God knows there's plenty of good cheap wine about today.' His *Guardian* obituary, written by Christopher Driver, another radical foodie, was headed: 'The people's wine is deepest red.'

Raymond Postgate, founder of *The Good Food Guide*, was jailed as a conscientious objector in the first world war, took to the picket lines in the General Strike and received a fan-letter from Lenin for his book on *The International During the War*. None of this was enough to save him from being regularly attacked by pious fellow-lefties for his gastronomic enthusiasms. 'Confounded nonsense,' he retorted. 'I should like to remind puritanical objectors that Major Cartwright, the first of the Reformers, was an expert on raisins and on gin and that Marx himself on occasion even got drunk.'

Just so: when Karl Marx had had a few he sometimes behaved in a manner more usually associated with Bertie Wooster on boat-race night. Engels, too, was a serious tippler who admitted that in 1848, the year of revolutions, he 'spent more time lying in the grass with the vintners and their girls, eating grapes, drinking wine, chatting and laughing, than marching'.

What Marx and Engels understood, even if some of their grim-faced followers didn't, was that there's nothing selfish and silly about shared pleasures, whether in the long grass or at the kitchen table. There are few things more conducive to comradeship than decent food and drink. It is, I think, no coincidence that the creator of the first top-class champagne was not some bloated plutocrat but Dom Perignon, a Benedictine monk of the 17th century who devoted his life to caring for the sick and needy. 'He loved the poor,' according to his epitaph, 'and he made excellent wine.' Note the conjunction: 'and', not 'but'.

Those who yearn for a better future need all the sustenance they can get. Pessimism of the intellect, Antonio Gramsci advised, must be accompanied by optimism of the will and how can one not feel optimistic at the sound of a popping cork, or the taste and texture of a perfect peach?

Francis Wheen, April 19 2000

* * *

Nouveau posh

It's so sweet that Posh Spice's hairdresser calls her 'Beaujolais', in a tribute to the lovely Chardonnay of

Footballers' Wives. What Mrs Beckham perhaps doesn't realise is that there could hardly be a naffer name. Beaujolais is in a deep slump. British wine merchants can't even shift the good stuff – and there is plenty of it, some of which they would almost pay you to take away.

Well, that's where greed gets you. The great beaujolais nouveau scam lasted for years until drinkers realised they were drinking a fluid which tasted as if it had just been drained from a sump. More and more wine was rushed to market, much of it well below standard, all to cash in on the fad. Now the vignerons are paying a terrible price. In the same way, German wine, much of which is delicious, is now paying for Blue Nun and Black Tower. Few people realise how good Portuguese reds are, because of Mateus Rosé.

If Victoria Beckham would like a really fashionable soubriquet, she might try 'Viognier', which is pretty, or the graceful 'Minervois'. 'Malbec' would be a good, tough, masculine name for their next son. Or if she really rates a mellifluous sound over vinous quality, I can't think of anything nicer than 'Hirondelle'.

Simon Hoggart, April 19 2003

* * *

Mad dogs and drunken Englishmen

The French, in my experience, are always shocked by the way we drink wine. There is no savouring of it. There is no allowing the liquid to mellow in the glass. None of that nose or palate thing, in other words; no ritual or even patience about it. It is a drug, a de-stresser, a soporific, the alcohol as blandly to hand as the water in the taps. On the very rare occasions that French people have been to dinner with us, I have seen them surreptitiously wide-eyeing each other across the table at the display their hosts are putting on for them. And that would be us on good behaviour, somehow deeply conscious that France is the centre of world civilisation and that we are heirs to a degraded northern version of it, which should, for shame, be concealed in front of them.

God only knows what they might think if they were to witness us on an average weekday, as the huge English middle-class wine-drinking habit swings into action: get home exhausted from work, open a bottle, slug a glass or three each, open another, feel still more exhausted – if by now pretty blunted – slump in front of the news and then crash out for a snory night, interrupted only by the need now and then to get up for a pee.

It is a weird and scarcely acknowledged fact that very nearly the entire nation ends its days in an alcohol-induced fug. Most of us never see it because we are in it, too. The strangeness of it struck me last year when I had to catch a train late at night from King's Cross in London. I had not touched a drop that evening and I arrived at the station to find the inhabitants of the capital wandering in a soft and befuddled way between the ticket office and the platforms, WH Smith and Burger King. It was as if the place were full of half-beings, semi-aware, semi-articulate, half-asleep, clumsy and, on that occasion, totally un-threatening, even rather sweet, like an exhausted pack of bleary old dogs staggering from the bed to the water bowl and back again, deeply loved by their owners but really not much good for anything else.

I know this is not exactly the violent aspect of alcohol currently exercising judges and the government, but it is intimately related to it. Immoderation may turn some of us into comatose labradors, but in others it releases the urge to aggression and violence. The key is in the quantity. A few sips of Pernod would not change behaviour in the way a skinful of Stella or a magnum or two of Jacob's Creek does. This is not something limited to a particular class. It affects all of us, so the deep and underlying question about the English and alcohol is not why we are aggressive when we are drunk, because not all of us are, but why we slug it back in such extraordinary quantities, which all of us do?

That is not a question that can be addressed by extending or shortening the opening hours of pubs and clubs. It would be difficult to think of anything more irrelevant. But it is the central conundrum. One answer may well be connected to the way in which we are all expected to behave. For all the upsurge of lad culture, the dominant ideal in English life remains nevertheless polite and conformist. For men in particular, in this country, it is not thought very good to be macho, at least not on a daily basis. We are not like the Europeans in that. The ideal Englishman is not a manly man with chest hair, predatory attitudes to women and a tough, domineering approach to other men. He is thought to be able to limit his vigour and manliness in a polite, self-deprecating, equable, charming, competent way, which does not loom over his surroundings but takes its place within them. The ideal English person is not tough but nice.

But that ideal comes at some psychological cost. The genuinely nice – the proto-labradors – may become labradors when drunk. But the would-be rottweilers become the real thing when tanked up. And the would-be rottweilers are those young men, in particular, who are not allowed in their everyday lives to express the manly, domineering behaviour that other more macho cultures might see as perfectly normal and natural.

The insistence on politeness actually creates the monster drunk. We are disastrously polarised about this, idealising a gentle vision of who we are, and, as a result, failing to accommodate the wilder, rougher and less attractive aspects of the aggressive self, which are either anaesthetised away in the nightly red wine coma, or released in horrible surges of alcohol-thick punching, kicking, knifing and killing.

Is there anything to be done? Perhaps not. The English have been famous in Europe as wild drinkers since the middle ages. The immoderation will continue. The only hope, maybe, is for more coma, less fighting.

Adam Nicolson, August 11 2005

* * *

LICENSING LAWS: OPEN TO CHANGE

Judges added their voice yesterday to the calls already made by police chiefs, medics and opposition parties for a slowdown in the introduction of more liberal licensing hours due in November. The 636-strong council of circuit judges, who have to deal with the consequences of binge drinking, spoke of the increase in serious assaults, domestic violence and disorder that extending drinking hours would produce. Like the medics, they wanted to see binge drinking addressed before more liberal hours were introduced. Otherwise, as one judge suggested yesterday, increasing the availability of the fuel that generates violence, would only produce more violence. They supported the government's goal of seeking to create a more civilised continental-style drinking culture, but noted that currently a significant minority of young people were intent on pursuing precisely the opposite approach, deliberately seeking to get drunk.

Ministers have some grounds for feeling miffed. Some five years ago they produced a white paper on licensing laws, designed to liberalise hours for the vast majority of sensible drinkers, but also deal with binge drinking. It set out a series of new police, court and local council powers to penalise pubs or wine bars that continued to serve people who were already drunk or whose customers caused public disorder. There was little serious objection to its main proposals. Three years ago a major licensing bill – the first for 100 years – followed the white paper's outline and passed into law. As late as last year, the police chiefs at their annual conference conceded that the new act would be 'a welcome and civilised approach to drinking' for the vast majority, but warned that dealing with binge drinking was 'beyond police capability' and the act could lead to more violence. Not much opposition was heard from the Conservative party, which liberalised afternoon drinking in the 1980s, until tabloid papers began a campaign of opposition to the new plan.

The act is now law. All sides want the same objective: less binge drinking. David Blunkett in an interview with the *Guardian* yesterday admitted that the new policy would have to be monitored and changed if it was a disaster. But why wait for a disaster before changing the ship's course? Given the strength of opposition, a sensible government – as we have argued before – would test its proposals in pilot schemes in a small number of towns. If they work, then let them proceed. Surely ministers have not forgotten Tony Blair's principle of policy-making: what matters is what works.

Leader, August 11 2005

* * *

WHO MADE CIDER COOL?

Last October, the analysts Mintel concluded that UK cider 'is in desperate need of a change of image to attract a wider and preferably younger consumer base'. A £1.2bn-a-year industry was becoming unprofitable, chiefly because of its close association with unsavoury seekers of personal oblivion. To that end, it didn't come as a surprise when the brewers Scottish & Newcastle withdrew its 'supersize' three-litre bottles of White Lightning and Symonds Original, each containing almost the maximum recommended weekly alcoholic intake.

Nearly a year on and home consumption of cider has risen by 20 per cent – extraordinary given the dearth of an international football tournament this summer, that usual catalyst for lucrative British boozathons. How did this happen? Have cider-drinking tramps and other unglamorous types risen by 20 per cent? Hardly. 'Cider has suddenly become the height of cool,' says Ian Targett, who, as Tesco's cider buyer, might be expected to say that. But he is not entirely wrong.

Two new brands, an Irish import called Magners and

the S&N-produced Strongbow Sirrus, have made Mintel's dream come true. They are ciders that the marketing johnnies insist should be poured from elegant bottles into flute or pint glasses and drunk convivially on the lawn at Glyndebourne. And, at only 4.5 per cent ABV, they will hardly turn you into your social circle's slurry pariah too quickly. 'What we've done,' says Maurice Breen, Magners' marketing manager in Clonmel, Co Tipperary, 'is try to normalise cider. In Ireland 15 years ago, cider had just the same bad connotations as it has had in Britain. In fact, we've used the same ads for the English launch as we did in Ireland, with the same Irish voice and the same notions of orchards and craftsmanship.'

Breen contends that his brand's unique selling point – pouring the stuff from a pint bottle into (be still, my revolted stomach!) a glass half filled with ice – 'was not a thinktank idea. It came from consumers 15 years ago in Ireland who knew that the drink had to be kept cold, but didn't really have proper refrigeration to do so.' Now, the TV ads (music: the Kinks' Summer Afternoon; vibe: smug ponces chilling) make a selling point of that practical solution to a drinking conundrum. Magners is selling well, Breen says. That is despite sceptics' misgivings about its greasy aftertaste and unnatural colour. But Breen shouldn't care what we think. His marketing triumph has made commercial cider too cool, and certainly too cold, for the likes of us.

Stuart Jeffries, August 30 2005

THE WORLD'S MOST DANGEROUS DRINKS

As Degas didn't say, absinthe is for wimps. So too is Jagermeister, ouzo, and other nasty spirits with top notes of a hen night in Lesvos and base notes of vomit. Whisky made from a 17th-century recipe and distilled four times to reach up to 92 per cent alcohol is proper, grown-up firewater. Jim McEwan, master distiller at the Bruichladdich distillery in western Scotland, was hard at it yesterday producing the first batch of what will be the world's strongest whisky when it is released in a decade or so.

It was known as 'the precarious whisky' 300 years ago because one tablespoonful would make you live for ever and two could make you go blind. 'If any man should exceed this, it would presently stop his breath, and endanger his life,' as writer Martin Martin explained in 1695.

How many spoonfuls has McEwan tried? 'I've had about six teaspoonfuls,' he says. It's 3pm and there are notes of happiness coming down the phone line. 'Not tablespoonfuls, so I'm fine.' What does it taste like? 'The nose was great. The texture was like satin, you know. There was tremendous power in it. The highest strength I got was 91.2 per cent. That was just too strong so I brought it down to 89 per cent and it was perfect. There were fantastic aromas coming from it. I was getting a fizzy lemon, almost a champagne effect, and then you got to the back of the palate and the alcohol hit.'

Steady on, Jim.

'It was quite leafy and mossy with notes of pine resin, hawthorn and rowan berries and afterwards it changed. I was getting more cereal notes like toasted rye bread. Then it was like walking through a field of clover. Other notes people were finding were toasted muffins and soft banana.'

Proof (and the Bruichladdich brew will come in at

178 degrees) that the whisky deserves a space in a cabinet of dangerous drinks. But what would sit alongside it?

Wormwood, the secret ingredient in the green fairy otherwise known as absinthe, contains thujone which, according to research quoted in Jad Adams's *History of the Devil in a Bottle*, 'excites the brain' by blocking chemical receptors that slow neural activity. Known as 'strangling the parrot', absinthe imbibing did, however, make Toulouse-Lautrec shoot at spiders plotting to attack him, and encouraged Hemingway to try 'knife tricks'. It was banned in France in 1915 after scares about its devastating effect on a third of the country's menfolk.

Norwegians fond of an illegal moonshine called hjemmebrent, said to be 96 per cent alcohol, make no such claims of creative thought. The writer Taras Grescoe found it purely functional. 'You were sober then you were drunk. It was grim, goal-oriented, and a little sad. And the hangover was like no other.'

Over to America, where Everclear sounds like a mouthwash but almost certainly tastes far worse at 190 degrees proof (95 per cent alcohol). Students find it blends most excellently with grape-flavoured Kool-Aid at house parties, where the spiritually-minded call it Purple Jesus. Mixed with Gatorade and Red Bull, it is called Crunk Juice; thrown together with the soft drink Mountain Dew it becomes Antifreeze.

Such crassness should not lead us to ignore the art of the special brew. 'It's like Neil Armstrong on the moon,' chuckled McEwan as he carefully watched over the distillation yesterday. 'It's wildly exciting.'

Patrick Barkham, February 28 2006

INVASION OF THE PUB SNATCHERS

Do New Yorkers know what they are letting themselves in for? That great city, where top-notch delis serve sandwiches the size of small central Asian republics, and where a good burger is never more than 20ft away, has welcomed its first gastropub. The Spotted Pig, run by the former River Cafe chef April Bloomfield, has opened in Manhattan to glowing reviews.

The initial delight of Manhattanites is understandable. When gastropubs started popping up around the UK a few years back, it seemed as if the face of the British gin palace had been changed for ever. We could say goodnight to dyspeptic landlords coughing into the beer and to reheated shepherd's pie served with crinkle-cut oven chips. Grime-encrusted frosted glass was smashed and replaced with huge picture windows, creating a new sense of security: you could check these pubs weren't the sole preserve of psychopaths with thousand-yard stares and a broken bottle in their hand before you walked in.

But what made those first gastropubs such a joy – the very fact they were different – has long since disappeared. The same establishments now constitute a 21st-century urban orthodoxy: they have become the Harvester restaurants of the middle classes. One gastropub was a delight, two was a choice, three is a bore.

Our cities now have too many boozers that appear to have been put together from a checklist of materials: mismatched chairs, wobbly tables, and beaten and cracked leather sofas. They employ staff who believe they are too educated or cool to serve the punters. They put a bunch of tasteful classic soul, reggae or chillout CDs on random play on the stereo. And the ubiquitous chalkboard menus offer the same handful of creaky classics from the gastro guidebook: char-grilled ribeye steak, seared tuna steaks, pan-fried chicken breast, oven-baked salmon (see previous complaint, but substitute baking for frying), probably finished off with a red-berry brulee.

Too many gastropubs have become convinced of their own innate superiority: ticking off the boxes on the checklist is enough of a guarantee of quality. They are encouraged in this notion by their gastro groupies – the trainer-wearing, baggy jeans-sporting young adults who fill them – who argue that the food might be the same in huge numbers of these places, but at least it is good.

Once, maybe, but not any more. In some sections of our cities – especially parts of London – the concentration of gastropubs is so great you can barely swing a cat without it being skinned, pan-fried and served up on a bed of puy lentils and rosemary. Simple logic suggests there cannot be enough good chefs to support such an array of eating places without a commensurate decline in their average quality.

What we are being served may not be the congealed lasagne that long dominated lunch menus, but it displays no more imagination, is often little tastier and is always three times the price. It was little surprise when the current edition of the *Good Pub Guide* revealed that the average cost of pub food has risen by nearly five times the cost of inflation in the past two years. Alisdair Aird, the guide's editor, was right to blame the wave of second-rate gastropubs.

The most upsetting aspect of this invasion of the pub snatchers, though, is how homogeneous our cafe society is becoming. As the self-styled gourmet burghers colonise our neighbourhoods, the choice of pubs becomes polarised: one can visit the gastropub or the scary pub. The middle ground of neighbourhood boozers where anyone could spend a couple of hours seems slowly to be disappearing.

In my own area I have seven gastropubs within 10 minutes' walk of my home. I have dozens of terrifyingly hard boozers. And I have just one classless, ageless pub where anyone from old man to young woman can feel comfortable. There was another – a really delightful backstreet pub, with the same few regulars at the bar every night, faded flock wallpaper, no music and a dartboard at the back – but that has been transformed. The old regulars have been displaced by young media workers, the silence by the sound of Groove Armada or some such, the old benches around the edge of the room replaced by the compulsory battered armchairs.

Can we not call time on the generic gastropub? I'm glad there are now pubs where one can get a half-decent meal, and some where the food is truly top-notch. I'm glad of the new cleanliness. I'm even willing to concede that 'pan' frying can produce better results than microwaving. But can we please set aside the notion that stripped floors and Czech lager are some mark of 'authenticity'?

Still, fashions will change. Mark my words: in two years' time the gastropub crowd will all be flocking to places with fruit machines, flat Carling Black Label and processed ham sandwiches made with curling Sunblest. So real, you see.

Michael Hann, April 28 2004

So now the experts say two glasses of wine a day is 'hazardous drinking'? I just don't believe it

It is a media tradition, indeed a journalistic necessity, to accompany scare stories about health issues with harrowing examples of people whose lives have been ruined by indulging in the unhealthy habit being described. Yesterday, the middle class was particularly singled out for a warning against 'hazardous' drinking. This, it turns out, is the stage you go through before getting on to 'harmful' drinking, which is what the bingers do. On the Today programme, Professor Mark Bellis, the chap in charge of the research commissioned by the Department of Health, explained that 'hazardous' drinking, for men, started at two bottles of wine a week – which is less than two ordinary glasses a day. For women, it's a bottle and a half a week.

I just don't believe that such amounts can be a realistic threat to health, so I looked in the papers for the customary human-interest story that is the warning to us all. ('I drank two glasses of wine a day and look at the wreck I've become,' etc.) I found none. Because, I suspect, there weren't any. I studied the examples given of nasty medical things that could happen, but they all seemed to relate to the risks of much heavier drinking. So was there any basis for the health warnings to the middle classes?

Bellis offered one: in effect, that a glass or two of wine a day could gradually turn into a daily bottle, which was too much. Yes, and the eater of one pizza a week may graduate to one a day. That is not an argument. I'm in favour of campaigns aimed at curbing the excessive consumption of alcohol, which encourages drinkers to violence and dangerous driving, as well as making them ill. What I'm against is scaremongering based on exaggeration. The government must not cry wolf about people's health. They run the risk of being disbelieved when they issue a warning on something that really does matter.

Marcel Berlins, October 17 2007

* * *

REASSURINGLY EXPENSIVE NO MORE

A person with a drink problem often tries to change the subject. Alcoholics would rather complain about stress at work or the demands of hectic socialising than think about the drinking itself. Something similar may be happening as Britain grapples with its own collective alcohol problem. Weekend figures from the World Health Organisation showed that the typical Briton now consumes the equivalent of 9.3 litres of pure alcohol a year, more than the average Russian. But rather than focus on how much is being drunk overall, the debate fixes on particular groups and particular patterns of drinking, as if these alone were the issue.

The volume of ink spilled on boozing ladettes rivals that of the Bacardi Breezers they swallow. Many young women, it is true, are doing themselves real harm – but no more so than many young men. Official figures released in January showed that men are drinking twice as much as women. Even allowing for higher male tolerance, that suggests men still have the more serious alcohol problem. Since the licensing law was relaxed in 2005, an alternative focus for the moral panic has been late-night drinking. Although the predicted crime wave never materialised, the anxiety reached such a pitch that Gordon Brown launched a review of the two-year-old laws during the first few weeks of his premiership. The review reports this week and – if Mr Brown's advance comments to yesterday's *Daily Mirror* are any guide – it will conclude that extended pub opening hours have had only a peripheral impact.

That is hardly surprising. It has long been apparent that the alcohol boom is not being driven by pubs, but by off-licence sales, which have more than doubled over the past dozen years. Rather than admit the review has led nowhere, the government is set to shift the focus on to underage drinkers, with proposals to close down shops that repeatedly supply them with liquor. The move is worth considering, though it will not make much of a dent in the wider problem of drinking. After all, it has been illegal to sell children drink since Edwardian times. The law will never be perfectly enforced, not least because many teenagers will always have older siblings and friends. Besides, dangerous drinking is no more confined to young people than it is to women. Last week one treatment centre suggested that alcoholism is spreading among pensioners.

From suburban tipplers to market-square bingers, problem drinkers are a varied lot. There are few policies that have any bearing on them all, though raising the price is certainly one. The dizzying choice of discounted drink – just as available in the aisles of the superior supermarkets as it is during happy hour at the local – is the culmination of three decades during which its relative cost has lagged behind earnings. Duty increases in next week's budget would be one way to try to reverse that trend, though the chancellor is unlikely to go for truly significant rises. That is not just because of the fear of the political backlash, powerful as that would be, but also because big tax rises might meet with more legal cross-border shopping in Europe as well as a rise in illegal smuggling.

An alternative approach is relaxing the cutthroat competition that produced such cheap alcohol in the first place. The existing law regards lower prices as an unalloyed blessing, fining stores that collude to avoid them. That perspective is the right one in markets where shoppers choose purely rationally. But rational economic man is no drinker. The enjoyment he derives from his purchases is never mixed with regret, warped judgment or addiction. Drink is one of life's pleasures, but it can also have all these effects. When it does, those who use it end up harming others – if only by damaging their own health to the point where the health service has to pick up the pieces. The freedom to drink must be defended, but it is a freedom that should be exercised at the right price.

Leader, March 4 2008

* * *

FRIENDLY BARMAIDS, COSY FIRES, BUT HARDLY A DROP TO DRINK

Writing in the *London Evening Standard* just after the war, George Orwell described his favourite pub. The Moon under Water was 'uncompromisingly Victorian', furnished in 'the solid comfortable ugliness of the 19th century'. It had three bars and in winter a fire burned in the grate of at least two of them. It had neither a radio nor piano and was always quiet enough to talk. The barmaids were middle-aged women who knew most of their customers by name and called everyone 'dear'. At the snack counter you could get cheese, pickles, mussels and liver-sausage sandwiches; the dining-room upstairs served a hearty three-shilling lunch of meat and two veg, with a jam roll to follow. The pub's special glory was its back garden, where in summer you could have a cider in the shade of the plane trees while children played on the swing or nipped into the public bar to fetch their parents more refreshment. The last was against the law, but by turning a blind eye the landlord had made the Moon under Water the kind of family gathering-place that pubs ought to be.

Of course, it didn't exist. Orwell knew a few pubs that had some of these attractive features but none that possessed all. None the less, the Moon under Water remains the most famous idealisation of the English pub. Among a certain generation or a certain tendency, most of its specific characteristics have taken on the meaning of 'a proper pub'. The popular longings that the essay contains have influenced all kinds of things – gastropubs, the Campaign for Real Ale (Camra), government legislation – in the 62 years since it was written.

This week I read it at lunchtime in a pub called the Florence only a few hundred yards from where Orwell lived in Canonbury Square, where the Moon under Water was probably imagined and typed. The Florence is named after Florence Street, which, because there is no Rome Street or Venice Street, I imagine was the name of its builder's wife. The new pub sign, however, has a sunny painting of the bridge across the Arno while a blackboard on the corner tries to engage passing trade by describing the Florence as 'the last traditional pub in Upper Street', its approximate location.

What does 'traditional' mean? In the Florence's case it meant a flat screen showing Sky Sports with the sound turned off, the Stones and Franz Ferdinand as the substitute noise. Bellows lay decoratively in a disused fireplace. A sign above the bar said that house wine was only £6.95 a bottle before 7.30pm. There were five other customers. I asked about food. 'It's a Thai menu,' the barman said, so I ordered prawn toast for £3.50 and a pretty but tired-looking woman, possibly Thai, brought it to the table piping hot from the microwave upstairs.

'Sweety shots' were advertised for £2. I asked about them. 'A vodka shot with a sweet flavouring,' the barman said. 'Like you can have a Malteser shot or a blackcurrant shot.' A smile passed between us that suggested my ignorance and his knowledge were both somehow ludicrous.

I don't mean to mock. The Florence promotes a grand Sunday lunch and may well be the nearest thing to a traditional pub in Upper Street. All that's left of the Hare and Hounds is a fine plaster relief of the hunt, the Royal Mail is a burger bar, the Mitre is shuttered, the King's Head can be discounted because it has a theatre attached, the Old Parr's Head became a branch in a chain of frock shops.

Leaving their glazed-tile walls and stone lettering as mementoes – the frock shop still advertises Luncheons Daily from the brewers Barclay Perkins and Co – pubs are closing everywhere. Particular categories have been slowly disappearing for decades: pubs in refashioned inner cities, pubs in country villages. But the present rate is estimated at four a day and the old explanations of shrinking demographics or ruthless brewers no longer apply.

In 1989 the government decided to break up the monopoly that operated when brewers owned or leased 80 per cent of Britain's pubs. The result was the 'pubco', companies such as Mitchells & Butlers, which own chains such as Harvester or All Bar One, a new tier of owners and managers between the brewers and the customer.

Many pubcos are in trouble for the usual modern reasons. They borrowed heavily against assets, which now, like house prices, are falling, because beer consumption is falling, especially in pubs. The pub trade can point to several reasons: the smoking ban, the 4p increase on a pint introduced in the last budget on beer which is already the most highly taxed in Europe (eight times as high as Germany's). But the main cause is the usual modern villain, the supermarket. A pint of Foster's on special offer at Tesco costs 58p against about £2.50 in a pub. Thirty years ago about 95 per cent of beer was bought in pubs as opposed to shops. Now the figure is nearly 50-50. According to Camra, some supermarkets are now selling beer more cheaply than bottled water.

Does it matter? Camra makes a case for pubs as singularly British institutions, embedded in our island story, which especially in the country and given the vanishing of churches and post offices have an important role as one of the few remaining places that bring people together.

But for the rest of us in towns and cities? Talking this over with my wife, I wondered why we never went to pubs.

'Pubs!' she said. 'Big cavernous places with a funny smell, dodgy toilets and bad food.' And, she might well have added, most of them fully committed to the young, to drink, to the young getting drunk.

Thirty years ago it wasn't like that. Pubs were filled with the old. I remember blundering one Sunday night into the Duke of Wellington across the road from my flat in Islington and finding the saloon filled with men and women (some in hats) singing The White Cliffs of Dover, as though a late all-clear had sounded in 1975. Now the Wellington is a £1.8m house, while the Florence tries to pay its way with Malteser shots.

Then again, the British pub seems always to have been in crisis. Camra was founded in 1971; Christopher Hutt's book, *The Death of the English Pub*, came out two years later. But long before then there was a feeling that pubs were not as they had been or should be. Orwell may have liked 'the solid comfortable ugliness' of Victorian interiors, but throughout the 1920s and 30s breweries and advertising men wanted to get pubs back to their Chestertonian past as taverns and inns and filled their Tudorbethan saloons with horse brasses and hunting prints. Then as now their reality, as opposed to their ideal form, was problematic. In 1927 Ernest Selley published a book called *The English Public House As It Is* that gives a good documentary account of drinking life. Unlike Orwell, Selley was an obscure figure, but his prose has a similar vigour. In a Midlands pub he was reminded of Hogarth: 'The women were the most degraded I have ever met. They were noisily obscene. One woman illustrated filthy tales about herself with bodily motions.'

What many people did in Selley's pubs was get drunk. Orwell's Moon under Water never mentions this possibility. It remains in our imagination as a place of amiable but only slightly intoxicated conversation, no music, shafts of noon sunlight striking a gantry of carved wood. Like Gilbert Scott phone boxes, such pubs do exist. I know one near Chancery Lane. The trick is to find it.

Ian Jack, April 12 2008

REFERENCES

Ayerst, David *Guardian: Biography of a newspaper* (Collins, 1971)

Barr, Andrew *Drink – A Social History* (Pimlico, 1998)

Boston, Richard *Beer and Skittles* (Collins, 1976)

Brown, Pete *Man Walks into a Pub* (Macmillan, 2003)

Cornell, Martyn *Beer – The Story of the Pint* (Headline, 2003)

Driver, Christopher *The British at Table 1940-1980* (Chatto & Windus, 1983)

Dunkling, Leslie *Guinness Drinking Companion* (Guinness World Records Limited, 1992)

Sandbrook, Dominic *Never Had It So Good* (Little, Brown, 2005)

Taylor, Geoffrey *Changing Faces: A History of the Guardian, 1956-88* (Fourth Estate, 1993)

CP Scott 1846-1932 – The Making of the Manchester Guardian (Frederick Muller Ltd, 1946)

The Guardian and Observer digital archive
    archive.guardian.co.uk/

The Newsroom Oral History Project
    www.guardian. co.uk/newsroom/

INDEX

absinthe 30–3, 52–3, 255
abstinence societies 46
Ace of Spades 107–8
adulteration of drink 43–5
advertising 228–31
Alcohol abuse 210, 260–2
alcoholics 204–7
alcopops 233–4, 239–41
Algerian whisky 182–3
America 42–3, 62, 92–6, 106
American Temperance
    Society 45–6
aphrodisiac beer 218–19
Arlott, John 179, 210
Australia
    opening hours 62
    wine 147–9

barmaids ban 35
Beaujolais 246–7
beer 184–8
    aphrodisiac 218–19
    beliefs about alcohol
      content 70
    brewing 157–9
    buns and 153–4
    declining popularity 134
    Nazis and 120–1
    non-alcoholic 81
    and politics 111–12
Beer Act 1830 19
Beerhouse Act 1830 12–13
beer shops regulations 19–21
BEF (British Expeditionary
    Force) 117–18

Bible Christian Church 46
binge drinking 250–2
Boston, Richard 179–80
bottles 103–6, 127
Bradford 169–70
breathalysers 171–2, 175–7
Brewers' Exhibition 47–9
British troops/forces 115–18,
    211–13
Buddhism 45
bumper 14

Cadiz, Oporto and Light
    Wine Association
    (Limited) 28
Cafe Communists 244–5
Camra (Campaign for Real
    Ale) 180–1
cap-removers 105–6
children
    under age drinking 58
    age of starting drinking
      238–9
    drunken 37–8
    giving beer to workhouse
      52
    sale of drink to 36
Children Act 1908 36, 58
cider 252–3
    myths 58–9
    non-alcoholic beliefs 70
claret 54–5
clerics 164–5
cocktail parties 87–8
cocktails 96–101

essentials of 97–8
popularity with women 99
pros and cons 96–7
social customs 99–101
Cointreau 228–9
consumption of alcohol 260–2

dance halls 141–6
dangerous drinks 253–5
David, Elizabeth 133, 135–6
Defence of the Realm Act (DORA) 61, 76–80
demon drink 162–4
De Musset, Alfred 52–3
dram drinking 17–18
drink restriction order 75–6
driving 139–40, 158, 201–3
drunkenness 89–90, 141–6, 236–7
drunks 204–7

early closing order 76–80
Eighteenth Amendment 93, 96, 106
elections and drinking 42–3
Engels, Friedrich 246
Everclear 255

financial issues 196–8, 260–2
First World War 61, 64–9
France
    absinthe 30–3, 62, 64–5
    wines of 1825 16–17

gastropubs 234–5, 256–8
gentlemen's clubs 87
Germany
    adulteration of drink 44–5
    wines of 1825 15–16

gin 11
Gin Doctor 22–3
gin shops regulations 20
Gladstone, William 35
glass 13
glasses, exploding 125–6
Gluck, Malcolm 234
glucose 44
Gott, Richard 179
Greasbrough social club 168–9
Greenock Radical Association 46
Gretna Tavern 82–4
Guardian readers drink dossier 193–5

Habitual Drunkards Act 49–50
hangovers 188–90
hazards of drinking 204–7, 259–60
Heineken 229–30
Hetherington, Alistair 134
hjemmebrent 255
home brew 110–11, 155
House of Commons 128–9
Hutchinson, Dr Robert 55
Hyde Park demonstrations 56–7
hypoglycaemia 203–4

Intoxication Liquor Act 61
Irish poteen distillery 26–8
Irish themed pubs 241–4
isinglass 15

King, John 50–2
King's glass 14

labelling 126–7
lager 48–9, 135
  brewing 157–8
  draught 181
  home-brewed 155
lager louts 209–10, 221–8
Lancashire drinks 110–11
Lancet 54–5
Lanty Slee's cave 138
Licensing Acts 56–7, 250–2
  1872 35
  1921 87
  1988 209
  2003 235
limits, alcohol 195–6
Lincolnshire 181–2
Lindsey, Charles 23–4
liquid lunches 203–4
Liquor Control Board 61
London, Whitsuntide in
  57–8

Macmillan, Harold 133
Maine Law 13, 23–6
Manchester Guardian 7–9
Manchester's drunkenness
  chart 89–90
marmalade tea 165–8
Martini 118
Marx, Karl 246
medicinal preparations
  140–1
mixtures 190–3
morning after 188–90
Moscow Mule 147
Murphy, Francis 37

NAAFI (Navy, Army and
  Air Force Institutes)
  117–18

National Trade Defence
  Association 56–7
Navy's grog 113
Nazis and beer 120–1
night clubs 80–1, 87
non-alcoholic beer 81
Notes on a Cellar Book 84–5
no-treating order 70–2

opening hours 62, 75–80,
  158, 209, 219–21, 235

Penguin Brewery 213–15
Perignon, Dom 103
Peterloo Massacre 7
port 17, 70
porter 11
Postgate, Raymond 245–6
poteen distillery 26–8
prohibition petition 1916
  87
pubcos 265
public houses
  changing 158, 210
  gastropubs 234–5, 256–8
  ideal 262–7
  new types 88
  themed 215–18, 241–4
  types of 258

quality of liquor 95–6

real ale 180–1
road-houses 106–10
Road Traffic Act 1967 158,
  202
rum 113
rum jelly 14–15
Russia, vodka prohibition
  62, 64–5, 72–5

Saintsbury, George 84–5
sake 62–4
Sardinian sherry 159–62
Saturday night scenes 38–42
Scott, Charles Prestwich 8,
  36–7, 62
Second World War 115
sherry
  parties 88, 112
  Sardinian 159–62
Single Bottle Act 13–14
social classes 93–4, 196–8
socialists 244–6
Soho 121–2
speakeasies 93, 95
stoupes 29, 30

Taylor, John Edward 7–8, 36
teetotallers 45–7, 50–2
temperance 35–6
  jubilee 45–7
  relativity of 69–70
  and the war 65–9
Thatcher, Margaret 199–201
tinctures 140–1
trade's demonstration 56–7

vermouth 118
vodka
  popularity of 147
  price increase 151–3
  prohibition in Russia 62,
    64–5, 72–5

war *see* First World War;
  Second World War
  whisky 122–3
  Algerian 182–3
  danger of 254–5
  Lanty Slee's cave 138

marmalade 165–8
  Scotch 129–31
Whitsuntide in London 57–8
wine cellar decline 91
wine(s)
  of 1825 15–17
  Australian 147–9
  boxed 183–4
  doctors, friends of 131
  duties 28–30
  Englishmen and 247–50
  and food 173–4
  hazards of 259–60
  House of Commons
    128–9
  in the kitchen 135–6
  Lincolnshire 181–2
  non-alcoholic 184
  popularity 133–5, 149–51
  and social class 196–8
  therapeutic effects of 137
  women drinking 173–4
  working men
    consumption 165
women and alcohol 39–41
  cocktail popularity 99
  wine 173–4
Women's Services 123–5
Woolton, Lord 115
working men's clubs 87,
  168–9
wormwood 255

young people
  drunkenness in 141–6
  prohibition in the US
    94–5
  return of to London
    101–2